Interpreting LISP

Programming and Data Structures

Second Edition

Gary D. Knott

Interpreting LISP: Programming and Data Structures

Gary D. Knott
Civilized Software Inc., Silver Spring, Maryland, USA

ISBN-13 (pbk): 978-1-4842-2706-0 ISBN-13 (electronic): 978-1-4842-2707-7
DOI 10.1007/978-1-4842-2707-7

Library of Congress Control Number: 2017944089

Cover image designed by Freepik

Managing Director: Welmoed Spahr
Editorial Director: Todd Green
Acquisitions Editor: Steve Anglin
Development Editor: Matthew Moodie
Technical Reviewer: Daniel Holden
Coordinating Editor: Mark Powers
Copy Editor: Mary Bearden

Distributed to the book trade worldwide by Springer Science+Business Media New York, 233 Spring Street, 6th Floor, New York, NY 10013. Phone 1-800-SPRINGER, fax (201) 348-4505, e-mail orders-ny@springer-sbm.com, or visit www.springeronline.com. Apress Media, LLC is a California LLC and the sole member (owner) is Springer Science + Business Media Finance Inc (SSBM Finance Inc). SSBM Finance Inc is a **Delaware** corporation.

For information on translations, please e-mail rights@apress.com, or visit http://www.apress.com/rights-permissions.

Apress titles may be purchased in bulk for academic, corporate, or promotional use. eBook versions and licenses are also available for most titles. For more information, reference our Print and eBook Bulk Sales web page at http://www.apress.com/bulk-sales.

Any source code or other supplementary material referenced by the author in this book is available to readers on GitHub via the book's product page, located at www.apress.com/9781484227060. For more detailed information, please visit http://www.apress.com/source-code.

Printed on acid-free paper

Contents at a Glance

About the Author vii

About the Technical Reviewer ix

Acknowledgments xi

Introduction xiii

■Chapter 1: LISP 1

■Chapter 2: The Atom Table and the Number Table 3

■Chapter 3: Evaluation 9

■Chapter 4: Some Functions and Special Forms 11

■Chapter 5: S-Expressions 17

■Chapter 6: Typed-Pointers 19

■Chapter 7: Pictorial Notation 23

■Chapter 8: More Functions 27

■Chapter 9: Arguments and Results Are Typed-Pointers 31

■Chapter 10: List Notation 35

■Chapter 11: More Special Forms 39

■Chapter 12: Defining Functions: λ-Expressions 43

■Chapter 13: More Functions 47

■Chapter 14: Defining Special Forms 53

■Chapter 15: The Label Special Form 57

■Chapter 16: The Quote Macro 59

■Chapter 17: More Functions 61

■Chapter 18: More About Typed-Pointers 63

■Chapter 19: Binding Actual Values to Formal Arguments 67

■Chapter 20: Minimal LISP 75

■Chapter 21: More Functions 77

■Chapter 22: Input and Output 83

■Chapter 23: Property Lists 85

■Chapter 24: What Is LISP Good for? 91

■Chapter 25: Symbolic Differentiation 93

■Chapter 26: Game Playing 101

■Chapter 27: The LISP Interpreter Program 109

■Chapter 28: Garbage Collection 135

■Chapter 29: The *lispinit* File, the *linuxenv.h* File, and the
Makefile File 139

■Bibliography 145

Index 147

Contents

About the Author vii

About the Technical Reviewer ix

Acknowledgments xi

Introduction xiii

■Chapter 1: LISP 1

■Chapter 2: The Atom Table and the Number Table 3

■Chapter 3: Evaluation 9

■Chapter 4: Some Functions and Special Forms 11

■Chapter 5: S-Expressions 17

■Chapter 6: Typed-Pointers 19

■Chapter 7: Pictorial Notation 23

■Chapter 8: More Functions 27

■Chapter 9: Arguments and Results Are Typed-Pointers 31

■Chapter 10: List Notation 35

■Chapter 11: More Special Forms 39

■Chapter 12: Defining Functions: λ-Expressions 43

■Chapter 13: More Functions 47

■**Chapter 14: Defining Special Forms** 53

■**Chapter 15: The Label Special Form** 57

■**Chapter 16: The Quote Macro** 59

■**Chapter 17: More Functions** 61

■**Chapter 18: More About Typed-Pointers** 63

■**Chapter 19: Binding Actual Values to Formal Arguments** 67

■**Chapter 20: Minimal LISP** 75

■**Chapter 21: More Functions** 77

■**Chapter 22: Input and Output** 83

■**Chapter 23: Property Lists** 85

■**Chapter 24: What Is LISP Good for?** 91

■**Chapter 25: Symbolic Differentiation** 93

■**Chapter 26: Game Playing** 101

■**Chapter 27: The LISP Interpreter Program** 109

LISP in C 110

■**Chapter 28: Garbage Collection** 135

■**Chapter 29: The *lispinit* File, the *linuxenv.h* File,
and the *Makefile* File** 139

■**Bibliography** 145

Index 147

About the Author

Gary D. Knott, PhD, is founder/CEO of Civilized Software Inc., the makers of the Mathematical and Statistical Modelling software MLAB.

About the Technical Reviewer

 **Daniel Holden** is a well-known C programmer with an interest in creative programming projects and the author of the C programming book *Build Your Own Lisp*. By day he works as a researcher developing tools using machine learning for automatic character animation and by night he enjoys writing short stories, creating digital art, and developing games.

Acknowledgments

I am thankful for the help of readers in shaping and debugging this material, and additionally, for the team at Apress, Steve Anglin, Mark Powers, and Matthew Moodie, and also the team at SPi Global, including Baby Gopalakrishnan, Raagai Priya Chandrasekaran, among others.

Introduction

I wrote this little book to help teach LISP to students in a course on data structures. Consequently, it contains a careful description of the data structures manipulated by LISP functions. LISP centrally depends on a linked-list data structure, which is one of the landmark features popularized, if not introduced, with the advent of LISP. This data structure and others, notably hash tables, are also used in constructing a LISP interpreter.

This book is intended to achieve several purposes. First, it is intended to be a gentle, but precise, introduction to the LISP language; second, it is intended to present a nontrivial LISP interpreter written in C that presents several "lessons" about programming in general and interpreter writing in particular; third, it is intended to introduce a bit of the "flavor" of programming in LISP, which is quite different in some ways from programming in a procedural language like C, where programs are built statement by statement. And all of this is to be done in a short space without copious, and possibly tedious, elaboration. This book is not intended to prepare the reader for using a particular LISP system, rather the focus is on the cultural contribution that LISP has made to the discipline of programming.

The study of LISP, coupled with the study of a LISP interpreter intended for exhibition, is of special interest to students in the areas of programming languages and computer architecture as well as data structures. Indeed, this book will be useful to students in all areas of computer science, as well as for autodidacts, professional programmers, and computer enthusiasts in a wide variety of fields. Although some "programming maturity" is assumed, the preserving reader can progress by developing such a foundation by means of parallel study and practice.

With parallel study, this book is intended to be accessible for a wide range of interested readers from high school students through professional programmers. I would very much like to see students use this book to help them understand LISP and how a LISP interpreter is crafted, and thus understand the concepts involved in building an interpreter for any language. The best way to proceed is to compile and run the C LISP interpreter, and then experiment by modifying it in various ways. I hope this book can help all who use it to develop an aesthetic appreciation of this elegant programming language.

And finally, since the LISP Interpreter C program provided in this book is a nontrivial program requiring careful study to understand it, this book, along with a book on C, should also be of use in learning or relearning the marvelous "Swiss army knife" programming of language C.

CHAPTER 1

LISP

LISP is an interesting programming language, and the ideas involved in building a LISP interpreter are equally interesting [McC79]. This book contains an introduction to LISP and it also contains the data structure details and the explicit code for a working LISP interpreter.

LISP is a programming language with unique features. It is conceptually interactive. Input commands are given one by one and the associated result values are printed out. LISP is an applicative language, meaning that it consists mainly of functional application commands. Besides functional application, there are forms of assignment commands and conditional commands written in functional form. In general, iteration is replaced by recursion.

The data values on which a LISP function may operate includes real numbers. Thus, an expression like 1.5 + 2 is a LISP statement, which means: type out the result of applying + to the arguments 1.5 and 2. In LISP, function application statements are always written in prefix form, for example, +(1.5, 2). Moreover, rather than writing $f(x, y)$ to indicate the result of the function f applied to the arguments x and y, we write $(f x y)$ in LISP, so $(+ 1.5\ 2)$ is the LISP form for 1.5 + 2. Finally, functions in LISP are usually specified by identifier names rather than special symbols. Thus the correct way to compute 1.5 + 2 in LISP is to enter the expression (PLUS 1.5 2), which will, indeed, cause 3.5 to be printed out. An expression such as (PLUS 1.5 2) is called a *function call expression*. LISP functions can also operate on *lists of objects*; indeed the acronym LISP is derived from the phrase LISt Processing.

LISP is commonly implemented with an interpreter program called the LISP Interpreter. This program reads LISP expressions that are entered as input and evaluates them and prints out the results. Some expressions specify that state-changing side-effects also occur. We shall describe below how a particular LISP interpreter is constructed at the same time that LISP itself is described.

There are a variety of dialects of LISP, including extended forms, which have enriched collections of functions and additional datatypes. We shall focus on the common core of LISP, but some definitions given here are not universal, and in a few cases they are unique to the version of LISP presented herein (GOVOL). The GOVOL dialect of LISP presented here is similar to the original LISP 1.5 [MIT62]; it is not as complex as the current most frequently used varieties of LISP, but it contains all the essential features of these more complex varieties, so that what you learn in this book will be immediately applicable for virtually every LISP dialect. (Look up the programming language *Jovial* to learn the meaning of GOVOL.)

© Gary D. Knott 2017
G. D. Knott, *Interpreting LISP*, DOI 10.1007/978-1-4842-2707-7_1

CHAPTER 2

■ ■ ■

The Atom Table and the Number Table

The LISP Interpreter program maintains several general data structures. The first data structure is a symbol table with an entry for every named data object. These named data objects are called *ordinary atoms*, and the symbol table of ordinary atoms is called the *atom table*. (The term *atom* is historical; that is the term John McCarthy, the designer of LISP [McC60][MIT62], used.) The atom table is conceptually of the following form:

	name	type	value	plist	bindlist
0					
1					
$\vdots$					
$n-1$					

The atom table has n entries, where n is some reasonably large value that is unspecified for now. Each entry in the atom table has a name field, which holds the atom name, for example: "PLUS" or "AXY". Each entry also has a value field for holding the current value of the atom and an associated type field, which is an integer code that specifies the datatype of the value of the atom. For example, the value of the atom "PLUS" is a built-in function, which is classified by the integer typecode 10. Each atom table entry also has a plist field and a bindlist field, which I will discuss later. (A *field* is just a term for a sequence of bits wherein a binary value can be stored; usually such bit fields are not complete computer "words." Of course a binary value includes everything dealt with within a computer.)

The second data structure is a simple table called the *number table* in which floating-point numbers are stored. Every input number and every computed number is stored in the number table, at least for the period of time it is required to be there. The number table is conceptually of the following form:

© Gary D. Knott 2017
G. D. Knott, *Interpreting LISP*, DOI 10.1007/978-1-4842-2707-7_2

	number
0	
1	
$\vdots$	
$n - 1$	

Since the floating-point numbers include a large complement of integers, there is no (immediate) reason, except, perhaps, for speed, to have integers provided in LISP as a separate datatype.

> **Exercise 2.1:** Precisely specify the set of integers that are expressible in floating-point format on some computer with which you are familiar.

> **Exercise 2.2:** Is there a good reason that the atom table and the number table have the same number of entries?

> **Solution 2.2:** No, there is no good reason for this. It can be easily changed if desired.

The datatype codes are:

1	undefined
8	variable (ordinary atom)
9	number (number atom)
0	dotted-pair (non-atomic S-expression)
10	builtin function
11	builtin special form
12	user-defined function
13	user-defined special form
14	unnamed function
15	unnamed special form

These datatypes are exactly the datatypes available in the version of LISP discussed here. The reason for the seemingly peculiar type codes will be apparent later; they are chosen so that the individual binary digits have useful meanings.

Do not assume that the LISP interpreter looks up atom table or number table entries by searching the appropriate table linearly from top to bottom; it is acceptable to imagine this is the case for now, but you will later see that there are faster ways to do such look ups.

There are two kinds of *atoms* in LISP. All atoms occur in either the atom table or the number table; *ordinary atoms* are entries in the atom table, and *number atoms* are entries in the number table.

An ordinary atom is like a variable in FORTRAN. It has a name and a value. The name is a character string that is kept for printing and input matching purposes. The value of an ordinary atom is a value of one of the types listed above. A number atom, which represents a real constant, also has a value; this value is the floating-point bitstring representing the number. The value of a number atom cannot be changed; a number atom is thus a constant.

An ordinary atom whose value is undefined is created in the atom table whenever a previously unknown name occurs in a LISP input statement. An ordinary atom whose value is undefined has an arbitrary bit pattern in its value field and the typecode 1 in its type field.

An ordinary-atom-valued ordinary atom in entry i of the atom table holds an index j of an atom table entry in its value field; the value of the entry i atom is then the entry j atom. The typecode in the type field of such an ordinary-atom-valued ordinary atom is 8.

A number-valued ordinary atom A in entry i of the atom table holds an index j of a number table entry in its value field. Entry j in the number table is where the number atom representing the number value of the ordinary atom A is stored. The type field of entry i in the atom table holds the typecode 9.

A number atom is created in the number table whenever a number that is not already present in the number table occurs in the input or is computed. Each distinct number in the number table occurs in one and only one entry. Similarly, an ordinary atom is created in the atom table whenever an ordinary atom occurs in the input or is otherwise generated, which is not already present in the atom table. Each distinct ordinary atom in the atom table is stored uniquely in one and only one entry.

An atom may be its own value! In particular, this is always the case for a number atom, which is always made to appear to have itself as its value in the sense that the result of evaluating the number atom named n is the corresponding floating-point bitstring, which is represented lexically and printed out as the identical name n or a synonym thereof. Since number atoms are constants, their names and values are consistently confused in this fashion. Note that a number atom has many synonymous names, for example, "1", "1.0", and "1." are all names of the same value.

Numeric constant names are strings of one or more digits with an optional embedded decimal point and an optional initial minus sign. Ordinary atom names are strings that do not contain an open parenthesis, a close parenthesis, a blank, an apostrophe, or a period and do not have an initial part consisting of a numeric constant name. (A *blank* character is also called a *space* character.)

As mentioned earlier, it is convenient to identify numbers with their corresponding number names.

> **Exercise 2.3:** Which of the strings A, ABcd, ++, A-3, -, B' C, and 3X are ordinary atom names?

> **Solution 2.3:** All of them are ordinary atom names, except B' C and 3X.

An ordinary atom can be assigned a value by means of an assignment operator called SETQ, which is provided in LISP. For example (SETQ A 3) makes the ordinary atom A a number-valued ordinary atom whose value is 3; any previous value of A is lost. The value of A after the assignment is the result value of the expression (SETQ A 3) and this value is duly printed out when the expression (SETQ A 3) is entered as a command. We perhaps should say that (SETQ A 3) makes A a number-valued ordinary atom whose value is the number named by 3. However, as mentioned earlier, it is convenient to downplay this distinction. We are protected from abusing number names, since LISP refuses to honor input such as (SETQ 3 4).

A *function* can be defined formally as a set of ordered pairs O; this is the usual means by which set theory is made to serve as a basis for mathematics in general. The set of elements D that constitute the first-component values is called the *domain* of the function, and the set of elements R that constitute the second-component values is called the *range* of the function. The domain is the set of possible input values and the range is the set of possible output values. These domain and range elements can be whatever is desired, including k-tuple objects; however, if (a, b) is a pair of the function O with domain D and range R, so that $a \in D$ and $b \in R$, then no pair of the form (a, c), with $c \neq b$, is a member of the set of ordered pairs O representing the function. For example, the binary addition function is $\{ ((x, y), z) \mid z = x + y \}$. The value of a function-valued atom is conceptually such a set of ordered pairs. Thus the ordinary atom PLUS is conceptually initialized to have the value $\{ ((x, y), z) \mid z = x + y \}$.

> **Exercise 2.4:** If O is a set of ordered pairs representing a function whose domain is D and whose range is R, does it follow that $O = D \times R$?
>
> **Solution 2.4:** Definitely not (except when the number of elements in R is 1).
>
> **Exercise 2.5:** Does $((1, 2), 3)$ belong to the binary addition function? How about $((2, 1), 3)$ and $((2, 2), 3)$? Is the binary addition function an infinite set?
>
> **Solution 2.5:** Yes, yes, and no. Yes, the binary addition function is an infinite set.
>
> **Exercise 2.6:** The set S whose elements are the ordered pairs of numbers appearing as the first components of the ordered pairs of the binary addition function is a set of ordered pairs. Is S a function?

All LISP computations are done by defining and applying various functions. There are two forms of functions in LISP: ordinary functions and special forms. A *special form* in LISP is just a function, except that the LISP evaluation rule is different for special forms and functions. Arguments of functions are evaluated *before* the function is applied, while arguments of special forms are *not* further evaluated before the special form is applied. Thus the value of a special-form-valued atom is conceptually a set of ordered pairs just as is the value of a function-valued atom. We also need one descriptor bit to tell if such a set corresponds to a function or a special form. The typecode value incorporates this bit of information. It is important for LISP to "understand" both ordinary functions and special forms. For a hint as to why this is, note that SETQ is a special form.

Every input statement to LISP is an atom or an applicative expression (function call expression) that is to be evaluated, possibly with side-effects, and the resulting value is to be printed out.

There are a number of particular ordinary atoms initially present in the atom table. One such atom is NIL. NIL is an atom-valued atom whose value is itself NIL. Another atom initially present is T, which is an atom-valued atom whose value is itself T. One purpose of NIL is to stand for the Boolean value "false," and T, of course, is intended to stand for the Boolean value "true." (You might think F would be a better symbol for "false," but John McCarthy was a minimalist.)

> **Exercise 2.7:** Look up George Boole and read about Boolean algebra.

The names of all the built-in functions and special forms, such as PLUS, are the names of ordinary atoms that were initially established in the atom table with appropriate initialized values. The values of these ordinary atoms are conceptually ordered pairs, but in truth, the value field of an atom whose value is a built-in function or built-in special form is either ignored or is an integer code used to determine which function or special form is at hand.

Thus if "NIL" is entered into LISP, "NIL" is the output. Similarly if "T" is typed in, "T" is the output. If "PLUS" is typed in, an infinite set of ordered pairs should be printed out, but this is represented by printing out the name "PLUS" and the type of the value of "PLUS" in braces instead, such as: {builtin function:PLUS}

> **Exercise 2.8:** Would it be better to say that if "PLUS" is typed in, a finite set of ordered pairs is printed out? Explain why or why not. Hint: for any particular computer, the set of floating-point numbers is finite.

As discussed earlier, numbers are entered in the number table as number atoms. The presented name is the symbol string of the number, and the value is the associated floating-point value. Only the value is stored in the number table, however. A suitable name is reconstructed whenever this name needs to be printed out. Thus, typing "3" into LISP results in "3" printing out, and a number atom with the value 3 is now in the number table.

If a previously unknown ordinary atom *x* is entered into LISP by typing its name, then "*x* is undefined" is printed out, and the atom *x*, with the typecode 1, and an undefined value then exists in the atom table. If x is again entered as input, "x is undefined" is printed out again.

> **Exercise 2.9:** What is the result of entering "(SETQ A 3)" and then "A"?

> **Solution 2.9:** "3" and then "3" again. Also the number atom "3" is now entered in the number table in some row j, and the ordinary atom A is entered in the atom table in some row k of the form ["A", 9, j, –, –]. Note the *value* of A is a data object of type 9. The atom "A" itself is an ordinary atom, which would be described by the typecode 8 if it were to appear as the value of some other atom.

CHAPTER 3

Evaluation

Let's denote the value of an atom or function call expression, x, by $v[x]$ from now on. The evaluation operator, v, defined here, is essentially embodied in the LISP Interpreter program.

When x is an ordinary atom, $v[x]$ is the data object specified in the value field of the atom table entry for x. The type of this data object is given by the typecode in the type field of the atom x. When x is a number atom, $v[x] = x$.

Exercise 3.1: What is PLUS?

Solution 3.1: PLUS is an ordinary atom.

Exercise 3.2: What is $v[\text{PLUS}]$?

Solution 3.2: $v[\text{PLUS}]$ is, conceptually, a set of ordered pairs. $v[\text{PLUS}]$ is *not* an atom.

Exercise 3.3: What does the atom table entry for "PLUS" look like?

Solution 3.3: It is a row of the atom table of the form ["PLUS", 10, α, –, –], where α is a private internal representation of the set of ordered pairs which is the value $v[\text{PLUS}]$ described by the typecode 10.

Exercise 3.4: Why is $v[\text{NIL}] = \text{NIL}$?

Solution 3.4: Because the NIL entry in the atom table, say entry j, is initialized as: ["NIL", 8, j, –, –].

Exercise 3.5: What is $v[3]$?

© Gary D. Knott 2017
G. D. Knott, *Interpreting LISP*, DOI 10.1007/978-1-4842-2707-7_3

Exercise 3.6: What is $v[\text{ABC}]$, where ABC has never been assigned a value by SETQ?

Solution 3.6: $v[\text{ABC}]$ is undefined.

A function call expression $(f x y)$ is evaluated in LISP by evaluating f, x, and y in order from left to right, that is, by computing $v[f]$, $v[x]$, and $v[y]$, and then producing the result of $v[f]$ applied to the arguments $(v[x], v[y])$. The value $v[f]$ must be a function. Note x and/or y may also be function call expressions (as may f), so this rule applies recursively.

A special-form call expression, such as $(s x y)$, is evaluated in LISP by evaluating s, which must result in a special form, and then produce the result value of $v[s]$ applied to the arguments (x, y). The only difference between a function application and a special form application is that the arguments of a function are evaluated before the function is applied, whereas a special form's arguments are not preevaluated.

The analogous definitions for the value of general k-argument function call expressions and special form call expressions, of course, hold.

Exercise 3.7: Write a careful definition of $v[(f x_1 x_2 \ldots x_k)]$ where $v[f]$ is a function and $k \geq 0$; be sure to specify the order of evaluation. Do the same when $v[f]$ is a special form.

CHAPTER 4

Some Functions and Special Forms

We can now state a few built-in LISP functions and special forms. We do not describe the results obtained when "illegal" input of various kinds is evaluated. Such behavior varies according to the implementation of the LISP interpreter. Following is a list of special forms and functions in LISP:

- SETQ: **special form with a side-effect**

  $v[(\text{SETQ}\, x\, y)] = v[x]$, after $v[x]$ is made equal to $v[y]$ as an initial side-effect. x must be an ordinary atom, necessarily with a nonnumeric name. The type of the value of x is changed to be the type of $v[y]$, with a special modification in the case where $v[y]$ is an unnamed function or unnamed special form, which will be discussed later. Any previous value of the atom x is lost.

  Note that it is almost always equally correct to say that $v[(\text{SETQ}\, x\, y)] = v[y]$, with the side-effect of assigning $v[y]$ to be the value of the atom x.

- QUOTE: **special form**

  $v[(\text{QUOTE}\, x)] = x$.

- PLUS: **function**

  $v[(\text{PLUS}\, n\, m)] = v[n] + v[m]$. $v[n]$ and $v[m]$ must be numbers.

- DIFFERENCE: **function**

  $v[(\text{DIFFERENCE}\, n\, m)] = v[n] - v[m]$. $v[n]$ and $v[m]$ must be numbers.

© Gary D. Knott 2017
G. D. Knott, *Interpreting LISP*, DOI 10.1007/978-1-4842-2707-7_4

- MINUS: **function**

  $v[(\text{MINUS } n)] = -v[n].\ v[n]$ must be a number.

- TIMES: **function**

  $v[(\text{TIMES } n\ m)] = v[n] \cdot v[m].\ v[n]$ and $v[m]$ must be numbers.

- QUOTIENT: **function**

  $v[(\text{QUOTIENT } n\ m)] = v[n]/v[m].\ v[n]$ and $v[m]$ must be numbers with $v[m] \neq 0$.

- POWER: **function**

  $v[(\text{POWER } n\ m)] = v[n] \uparrow v[m]$ where $a \uparrow b$ denotes 'a to the power b', a^b; $v[n]$ and $v[m]$ must be numbers such that if $v[n] < 0$ then $v[m]$ is an integer.

- FLOOR: **function**

  $v[(\text{FLOOR } n)] = \lfloor v[n] \rfloor$, the greatest integer less than or equal to $v[n].\ v[n]$ must be a number.

- EVAL: **function**

  $v[(\text{EVAL } x)] = v[v[x]]$.

Exercise 4.1: Since $v[(\text{EVAL } x)] = v[v[x]]$, why doesn't $(\text{EVAL } x) = v[x]$?

Solution 4.1: Because the inverse of the evaluation operator v does not exist.

Exercise 4.2: Suppose the atom A has never been assigned a value via SETQ. What is $v[(\text{QUOTE } A)]$? What is $v[A]$?

Solution 4.2: $v[(\text{QUOTE } A)] = A$, but $v[A]$ is undefined. Note $v[v[(\text{QUOTE } A)]] = v[A]$, so $v[(\text{EVAL } (\text{QUOTE } A))] = v[A]$ whether A has a defined value or not; EVAL acts as the left-inverse of QUOTE, or equivalently, QUOTE acts as the right-inverse of EVAL.

Exercise 4.3: What is $v[(\text{PLUS } (\text{QUOTE } 3)\ 2)]$?

Solution 4.3: 5, since $v[x] = x$ when x is a number.

Exercise 4.4: What does (SETQ T NIL) do?

Solution 4.4: NIL is the output, and the value of T is now changed to be NIL.

Most versions of LISP have ways of specifying that the value of an atom is constant and cannot be changed. We will not introduce this complication here, but obviously, it is perilous or worse to assign new values to important ordinary atoms like NIL.

Exercise 4.5: What is $v[(\text{SETQ } (\text{SETQ } A\ T)\ (\text{SETQ } B\ \text{NIL}))]$?

Solution 4.5: An error arises, since the first argument to the outer SETQ is not an ordinary atom. Remember, $v[\text{SETQ}]$ is a special form.

Exercise 4.6: What does (SETQ P PLUS) do?

Solution 4.6: Now $v[P] = v[\text{PLUS}]$, so now $v[(P\ 2\ 3)] = 5$. Also "{builtin function: P}" is printed out.

Exercise 4.7: What does (SETQ PLUS −1.) do?

Solution 4.7: The function value of PLUS is discarded, and now $v[\text{PLUS}] = -1$. Also −1 is printed out.

Note that SETQ is a special form, yet its second argument is evaluated. It is more correct to say that SETQ is passed its arguments, and then *it* performs the required computation, which entails computing the value of the supplied second argument. Thus special forms may selectively evaluate some or all of their arguments, but such evaluation, if any, is done *after* the arguments are passed to the special form.

Note that not all LISP functions are defined for all possible LISP data objects occurring as input. A function that does accept any input is called a *total* function. The function TIMES, for example, only accepts numbers as input. The function EVAL may appear to be a total function, but consider $v[(\text{EVAL } \text{PLUS})]$. This is $v[v[\text{PLUS}]]$, where $v[\text{PLUS}]$ is a set of ordered pairs. But the v-operator value of a set of ordered pairs is not, thus far, defined. $v[(\text{EVAL } (\text{QUOTE } \text{PLUS}))]$ is defined, however, and we can make LISP a little less persnickety by defining $v[x] = x$ when x is a function or special form. We will adopt this extension henceforth. Then $v[(\text{EVAL } \text{PLUS})] = v[(\text{EVAL } (\text{QUOTE } \text{PLUS}))]$.

Exercise 4.8: Even with the just introduced convention, EVAL is not a total function. Give an example of illegal input to EVAL.

Solution 4.8: The input A, where A is an atom whose value is undefined, is illegal input to EVAL. Later, when dotted-pairs are introduced, we will see that input like (3 . 5) is illegal also.

Exercise 4.9: What happens if "v[NIL]" is typed in to the LISP Interpreter?

Solution 4.9: An atom whose name is "v[NIL]" is specified and its value (which is probably undefined) is printed out. The v-operator is *not* a LISP function. It *is* the LISP Interpreter and hence is more properly called a meta-operator.

A *predicate* is a function whose result values are always the Boolean values *true* or *false*. In the case of LISP, the result value of a predicate is always either T or NIL. We identify functions as predicates merely for descriptive convenience. This explains the choice of the names NUMBERP and ZEROP defined below. Not every LISP predicate follows this naming convention, however; for example EQ, defined below, is a predicate. Following is a list of LISP predicates:

- EQ: **predicate**

  v[(EQ x y)] = if v[x] = v[y] then T else NIL where v[x] and v[y] are atoms. Although, strictly, v[x] and v[y] must be atoms, nonatoms may well work in certain circumstances.

- NUMBERP: **predicate**

  v[(NUMBERP x)] = if v[x] is a number then T else NIL.

- ZEROP: **predicate**

  v[(ZEROP x)] = if v[x] = 0 then T else NIL.

Exercise 4.10: What is v[(EQ 2 (SETQ B 3))]?

Solution 4.10: NIL, and now v[B] = 3 due to the assignment side-effect.

Exercise 4.11: What is v[(EQ .33333 (QUOTIENT 1 3))]?

Solution 4.11: Probably NIL, since 1/3 ≠ .33333; but possibly T if the precision of floating-point numbers is less than 6 decimal digits. All the usual vagaries of floating-point arithmetic are present in LISP.

Exercise 4.12: What is $v[$(EQ (NUMBERP 0) (ZEROP 0))]$?

Solution 4.12: T.

Exercise 4.13: Is EQ a total function?

Exercise 4.14: What is $v[$(ZEROP (PLUS 2 (MINUS 2)))]$?

Solution 4.14: It is T. Because $v[$(PLUS 2 (MINUS 2))$] = v[2] + v[$(MINUS 2)$] = 2 + (-v[2]) = 2 + (-2) = 0$.

Exercise 4.15: What is $v[$(EQ 0 NIL)]$?

Solution 4.15: NIL.

Exercise 4.16: Why are capital letters used for ordinary atom names in this book?

Solution 4.16: Only for the sake of uniformity and tradition. Lowercase letters are perfectly acceptable within ordinary atom names, along with many special characters.

CHAPTER 5

■ ■ ■

S-Expressions

LISP has built-in functions that deal with certain composite data objects constructed out of atoms. These data objects are called *nonatomic S-expressions*. They are binary trees whose terminal nodes are atoms. Some of these trees can be interpreted as *lists*, and these are a very popular form in LISP. Indeed, as mentioned earlier, LISP derives its name from the phrase "list processing." Atoms and nonatomic S-expressions, taken together, form the class of data objects whose members are called *S-expressions*. The term *S-expression* is short for the phrase symbolic expression. Nonatomic S-expressions play the role of arrays in other programming languages.

The class of S-expressions is defined syntactically as follows. Every atom is an S-expression, and, if *a* and *b* are S-expressions, then the *dotted-pair* (*a*. *b*) is an S-expression. Mathematically speaking, a dotted-pair is merely an ordered pair. Note dotted-pairs *must* be enclosed in parentheses. The terms *nonatomic S-expression* and *dotted-pair* are synonymous.

Thus, for example, all the following expressions are S-expressions, and the last five are nonatomic S-expressions. (Note some of these S-expressions are, by themselves, legal LISP input and some are not.)

```
T
NIL
3
(1 . T)
((0 . .1) . NIL)
(((1 . 2) . (3 . 4)) . 5)
(PLUS . A)
(PLUS . (1 . (2 . NIL)))
```

Dots are *not* operators; dots and parentheses are merely used to give a concrete form to the abstract idea of dotted-pairs in exactly the same way that digit symbols are used to provide a concrete form for the abstract idea of integers. Dots and parentheses are used within *dot notation* in LISP parlance.

Exercise 5.1: Is (A . (B . C) . D) an S-expression?

Solution 5.1: No. Every dot must be used to form a dotted-pair, and every dotted-pair must be enclosed in parentheses.

© Gary D. Knott 2017
G. D. Knott, *Interpreting LISP*, DOI 10.1007/978-1-4842-2707-7_5

Exercise 5.2: How can dots be used as decimal points in numbers and also as the connectors in dotted-pairs without confusion?

Solution 5.2: Dots used as decimal points must appear immediately adjacent to one or two digit characters; a dot used as a dotted-pair connector must have one or more blanks intervening between it and a digit.

Exercise 5.3: How many S-expressions are there?

Solution 5.3: In any LISP program only a finite number of S-expressions arise, but conceptually, the set of S-expressions has an infinite number of members. In fact, the set of ordinary atoms, by itself, has an infinite number of members.

The special form QUOTE is used to specify constant S-expressions. A number, like 1.5, is a constant by virtue of the convention that it is self-referentially defined, so that $v[1.5] = 1.5$. However, the dotted-pair (T . NIL) or the atom A denote their values in most contexts, so if we wish to prevent such possibly foolish evaluations, we must write (QUOTE (T . NIL)) or (QUOTE A).

Exercise 5.4: What is $v[(\text{QUOTE } 3)]$?

Exercise 5.5: Suppose (SETQ A 3) is typed into the LISP Interpreter. Explain how the LISP Interpreter computes $v[A]$ in the course of executing (SETQ A 3), that is, in the course of computing $v[(\text{SETQ } A 3)]$. Compare this with the evaluation of A that is required when A is entered as input. Construct a fragment of a program in a conventional language like C to aid in this explanation.

CHAPTER 6

■ ■ ■

Typed-Pointers

Internally, that is, inside the computer, an ordinary atom in LISP is represented by an integer index into the atom table, that is, by a pointer. We use the terms *index* and *pointer* interchangeably as seems fit; the term *address* is sometimes used as well. By knowing a pointer to an ordinary atom, we can access both the name and the value of the atom. A number atom is represented by an integer index into the number table where the corresponding floating-point value is stored.

Similarly a nonatomic S-expression is also represented internally by a pointer. Some means are needed in order to distinguish what kind of object a pointer points to. Thus we shall carry an integer typecode with a pointer and refer to the pair together as a *typed-pointer*.

A typecode and pointer, which together form a typed-pointer, will be packed into one 32-bit computer word. Thus a typed-pointer consists of two adjacent bit fields that form a 32-bit integer. The first 4 leftmost bits hold the type of the pointed-to data object, and the remaining 28 rightmost bits hold the pointer or index to the pointed-to data object. We assume a traditional binary integer representation where the high (leftmost) bit determines the sign of the combined number stored in a 32-bit computer word, with 0 indicating a nonnegative integer and 1 indicating a negative integer. A typed-pointer that forms a nonpositive 32-bit integer will be a pointer to an ordinary atom in the atom table, to a number atom in the number table, or will be, as we will discuss later, a pointer to a function or special form. A typed-pointer that forms a positive integer will be a pointer to a dotted-pair.

> **Exercise 6.1:** Can we choose a different size, say 48 bits, for typed-pointers in order to allow bigger collections of S-expressions to be constructed?
>
> **Solution 6.1:** No, *we* can't, but the programmers building a LISP Interpreter can.

In fact, the type-field and the value-field in each atom table entry are packed in a single 32-bit word that can be easily accessed as a typed-pointer.

We will use the integers in $\{1, 2, \ldots, m\}$ as pointers (indices) to nonatomic S-expressions. In fact, we establish an array of structures: $P[1:m]$(integer car, cdr), called the *list area*, and each nonatomic S-expression pointer j is interpreted as an index into P.

© Gary D. Knott 2017
G. D. Knott, *Interpreting LISP*, DOI 10.1007/978-1-4842-2707-7_6

An element of P is called a *list node*. The integers *car* and *cdr* that make up the element P_j are called *fields* of P_j. The declaration notation above is intended to indicate that each list node P_j consists of a pair of integer fields: $P_j.car$ and $P_j.cdr$.

Note that the atom table and the number table each have n entries with their indices ranging from 0 to $n-1$, and the list area has m entries with indices ranging from 1 to m. The values n and m have values determined by the programmers of the LISP Interpreter.

The typecodes used in typed-pointers are:

  0000: dotted-pair (nonatomic S-expression)

  0001: undefined

  1000: variable (ordinary atom)

  1001: number (number atom)

  1010: builtin function

  1011: builtin special form

  1100: user-defined function

  1101: user-defined special form

  1110: unnamed function

  1111: unnamed special form

Thus, because the sign-bit of the 32-bit computer word is the leftmost bit of the typecode field, a typed-pointer t with $t > 0$ points to a dotted-pair, and a typed-pointer t with $t < 0$ points to other than a dotted-pair. (A typed-pointer with the typecode 0001 is a positive value, but it occurs only in the atom table and will never arise in the context where we expect a typed-pointer referring to a dotted-pair.)

> **Exercise 6.2:** What do the individual bits of the typecode values indicate?
>
> **Solution 6.2:** Numbering the bits as 1, 2, 3, etc., from left to right, we see that bit 1 is 0 for a dotted-pair (or an undefined value), and bit 1 is 1 otherwise. Within the class of function and special form typecodes, bit 2 is 0 for a builtin function or special form, and bit 2 is 1 otherwise; and bit 4 is 1 for a special form and bit 4 is 0 for a function. This bit-encoding is harmless, but it isn't really very important or very useful; arbitrary numbers would be nearly as convenient.

If j is a 28-bit untyped-pointer, that is, a simple address or an index, then the following functions may be used to form a typed-pointer, where :: denotes bit-string concatenation. These functions are *not* LISP functions that are predefined in LISP; they are convenient meta-functions, which allow us to describe the internal form and meaning of the LISP Interpreter program. Some examples are:

$$se(j) = 0000 :: j$$
$$oa(j) = 1000 :: j$$
$$nu(j) = 1001 :: j$$
$$bf(j) = 1010 :: j$$
$$bs(j) = 1011 :: j$$
$$uf(j) = 1100 :: j$$
$$us(j) = 1101 :: j$$
$$tf(j) = 1110 :: j$$
$$ts(j) = 1111 :: j$$

Now we can explain how any particular nonatomic S-expression is represented. If j points to a nonatomic S-expression of the form (B . C), then $P_j.car$ points to the S-expression B and $P_j.cdr$ points to the S-expression C. Note that B or C or both may be atomic S-expressions; this just means the corresponding typed-pointer may not be positive.

> **Exercise 6.3:** Is the 32-bit value 0 a legal typed-pointer? If so, what does it point to? What about the 32-bit value 1?

CHAPTER 7

■ ■ ■

Pictorial Notation

Let us suppose the atom table and the number table are loaded as follows:

	name	type	value		
0	NIL	8	0	0	.5
1	T	8	1	1	1.6
2	PLUS	10	–		
3	X	9	0		
4	Y	9	0		
5	Z	1	–		
6	QUOTE	11	–		

atom table: number table:

Then X is represented by the typed-pointer $oa(3)$ and NIL is represented by the typed-pointer $oa(0)$, both of which are negative integers. Remember that the type field in an atom table entry describes the type of the *value* of that ordinary atom. The S-expression (T . NIL) is represented by a positive integer j such that $P_j.car = oa(1)$ and $P_j.cdr = oa(0)$; that is (T . NIL) corresponds to j where $P_j = (oa(1), oa(0))$. Note $se(j) = j$.

We shall write the name of an atom in the *car* or *cdr* field of a pictorially given list node to indicate that a nonpositive typed-pointer to that atom is there. Thus (T . NIL) corresponds to j where $P_j =$ | T | NIL |. This is intended to be a pictorial representation of the two integer fields that form the list area structure element P_j. Number atom names are used similarly. Thus (2 . 3) is represented by an integer j such that $P_j =$ | 2 | 3 |. This means that $P_j.car$ is a negative integer x whose low 28 bits indexes the number atom 2 in the number table and $P_j.cdr$ is a negative integer y whose low 28 bits indexes the number atom 3 in the number table, so that $P_j = (x, y)$. The high four bits of x and y in this case are both 1001.

The S-expression ((PLUS . X) . (X . NIL)) is represented by a pointer j, where $P_j = (a, b)$ and $P_a = \boxed{\text{PLUS} \quad \text{X}}$ and $P_b = \boxed{\text{X} \quad \text{NIL}}$. This, of course, means that for the example atom table above, $P_a.car = oa(2)$, $P_a.cdr = oa(3)$, $P_b.car = oa(3)$, and $P_b.cdr = oa(0)$. Rather than introduce the intermediate pointers a and b by name, we usually will show the same structure pictorially as:

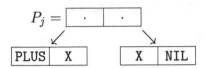

As another example, the S-expression (NIL . (((X . T) . NIL) . (T . T))) is represented by a pointer k, where:

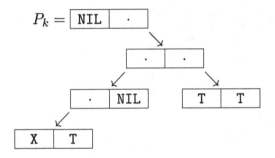

The following exercises assume the same example atom table used just above.

Exercise 7.1: What pointer represents $v[(\text{QUOTE PLUS})]$?

Solution 7.1: $oa(2)$.

Exercise 7.2: What pointer represents .5?

Solution 7.2: $nu(0)$.

Exercise 7.3: What pointer represents $v[(\text{PLUS X X})]$?

Solution 7.3: We can't say exactly, but the result is the number 1, which is a number atom not shown above, so it must be a nonpositive integer of the form $nu(j)$ for some integer $j > 1$.

Exercise 7.4: What is the S-expression represented by $se(3)$, where $P_3 = (se(1), oa(0))$ and $P_1 = (oa(1), se(2))$ and $P_2 = (oa(6), oa(6))$?

Solution 7.4: ((T . (QUOTE . QUOTE)) . NIL).

Exercise 7.5: Is there any confusion between $oa(3)$ and $se(3)$?

Solution 7.5: No.

Exercise 7.6: What is the pictorial representation of (((X . NIL) . NIL) . NIL)?

Exercise 7.7: What is the pictorial representation of (X . (Y . (Z . NIL) . NIL) . NIL)?

Solution 7.7: None. This is not a legal S-expression.

Exercise 7.8: What is the S-expression represented by the typed-pointer $oa(5)$?

Solution 7.8: Z.

Exercise 7.9: What is the S-expression represented by the positive integer j where:

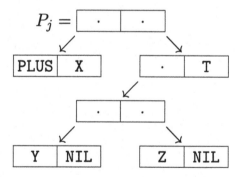

Exercise 7.10: Explain why nonatomic S-expressions can be described as binary trees whose terminal nodes are LISP atoms. How can the nonterminal nodes be characterized? Are there any structural constraints on the form of the binary trees that correspond to nonatomic S-expressions?

Exercise 7.11: What kinds of typed-pointers may occur in the car or cdr fields of an S-expression?

Solution 7.11: Dotted-pair (0000), ordinary atom (1000), and number atom (1001) typed-pointers comprise the only kinds of typed-pointers that appear in S-expressions.

CHAPTER 8

More Functions

Here we present some basic functions in LISP that operate on nonatomic, as well as atomic, S-expressions.

- ATOM: **predicate**

  $v[(\text{ATOM } x)] = $ if $v[x]$ is an ordinary atom or a number then T else NIL.

- CONS: **function**

  $v[(\text{CONS } x\,y)] = (v[x] \; . \; v[y])$. x and y are arbitrary S-expressions. CONS is the dotted-pair construction operator.

- CAR: **function**

  $v[(\text{CAR } x)] = a$ where $v[x] = (a \; . \; b)$ for some S-expressions a and b. If $v[x]$ is not a nonatomic S-expression, then (CAR x) is undefined, and any result is erroneous.

- CDR: **function**

  $v[(\text{CDR } x)] = b$ where $v[x] = (a \; . \; b)$ for some S-expressions a and b. If $v[x]$ is not a nonatomic S-expression, then (CDR x) is undefined, and any result is erroneous.

The basic relation among CONS, CAR, and CDR is:

$$v[(\text{CONS } (\text{CAR } x) \; (\text{CDR } x))] = v[x]$$

© Gary D. Knott 2017
G. D. Knott, *Interpreting LISP*, DOI 10.1007/978-1-4842-2707-7_8

where $v[x]$ is a nonatomic S-expression. The CONS function constructs a dotted-pair, the CAR function returns the first member of a dotted-pair, and the CDR function returns the second member of a dotted-pair.

> **Exercise 8.1:** Is the relation among CONS, CAR, and CDR characterized by the statements: $v[(\text{CAR } (\text{CONS } x\,y))] = v[x]$ and $v[(\text{CDR } (\text{CONS } x\,y))] = v[y]$?

Names such as FIRST and TAIL would be more descriptive than CAR and CDR. The names CAR and CDR stand for the phrases "contents of the address register" and "contents of the decrement register," respectively. They arose because the first implementation of LISP programmed in 1958 was done for an IBM 704 computer in which each list node was held in one 36-bit computer word. The single word instructions of the 704 had a format consisting of a (divided) op-code field, a decrement field, and an address field, and in list nodes, these latter two fields were used for the second and first pointers, respectively, of a dotted-pair. The word *register* was used instead of *field* because these address fields could be efficiently loaded into registers on the 704.

> **Exercise 8.2:** Show how the names FIRST and TAIL can be used in place of the names CAR and CDR. Hint: use SETQ.

> **Exercise 8.3:** Shouldn't the *car* and *cdr* fields in the list area elements P_i be called the *ar* and *dr* fields instead?

> **Exercise 8.4:** What is $v[(\text{CONS NIL T})]$?
>
> **Solution 8.4:** (NIL . T).

> **Exercise 8.5:** What does the name CONS stand for?
>
> **Solution 8.5:** It stands for the word "construction."

> **Exercise 8.6:** What is $v[(\text{CONS } (\text{CDR } (\text{CONS NIL T}))$ $(\text{CAR } (\text{CONS NIL T})))]$?
>
> **Solution 8.6:** (T . NIL).

> **Exercise 8.7:** What is $v[(\text{CAR PLUS})]$?
>
> **Solution 8.7:** Undefined. (By *undefined*, we mean undetermined; we haven't said what the evaluation operator v does with such input. Strictly, you might imagine that the evaluation of an illegal input expression results in "illegal input" being printed out.)

Exercise 8.8: What is $v[$(CONS PLUS 3)$]$?

Solution 8.8: Undefined, because $v[$PLUS$]$ is not an S-expression! (Go back and check the definition of an S-expression.)

Exercise 8.9: What is $v[$(CONS (QUOTE QUOTE) (QUOTE PLUS))$]$?

Solution 8.9: (QUOTE . PLUS).

Exercise 8.10: What is $v[$(ATOM NIL)$]$? What is $v[$(ATOM (QUOTE NIL))$]$? What is $v[$(ATOM (QUOTE (QUOTE . NIL)))$]$?

Solution 8.10: (1) T, (2) T, and (3) NIL.

Exercise 8.11: What is $v[$(ATOM 12.5)$]$?

Solution 8.11: T.

Exercise 8.12: What is $v[$(ATOM PLUS)$]$?

Solution 8.12: NIL. Because $v[$PLUS$]$ is a function, that is, a set of ordered pairs, it is *not* an atom.

Exercise 8.13: We said that nonatomic S-expressions were binary trees. Consider the LISP code: (SETQ A (CONS T (QUOTE B))) (SETQ B (CONS (CONS A A) (CONS (QUOTE B) A)). Diagram the resulting nonatomic S-expression value of B. Note the sharing of the S-expression $v[$A$]$!

CHAPTER 9

■ ■ ■

Arguments and Results Are Typed-Pointers

Internally in the LISP Interpreter program, callable LISP functions and special forms take typed-pointers to S-expressions as input and return a typed-pointer to an S-expression as output. The only (apparent) exceptions are those functions and special forms that accept or return functions or special forms, that is, conceptually sets of ordered pairs. In fact, typed-pointers will be used in these cases as well. When a result is computed, a typed-pointer to that result S-expression or function is returned. When the final result is computed, the typed-pointer to the final result is used to reach the pointed-to data object, which is then inspected in order to print out its complete lexical representation as the final deliverable.

We can now describe the workings of some of the functions and special forms defined before.

For (QUOTE x), v[QUOTE] receives as input a typed-pointer to an S-expression x, and the same typed-pointer is returned as the result.

For (PLUS $x\,y$), v[PLUS] receives two typed-pointers as input, one to $v[x]$ and one to $v[y]$ (remember, by the rules of LISP, v[PLUS] is a function, so x and y get evaluated before v[PLUS] is called). If the two typed-pointers received by v[PLUS] do not both point to number atoms, PLUS is being used erroneously. Otherwise, the sum value is formed and a number atom with the corresponding floating-point value is formed. A typed-pointer to this number atom in the number table is the result.

For (EQ $x\,y$), v[EQ] receives two typed-pointers as input: one to $v[x]$ and one to $v[y]$. If these two typed-pointers are identical, a typed-pointer to the atom T is returned, otherwise a typed-pointer to the atom NIL is returned. Thus EQ will correctly report whether or not two atoms are equal, since atoms are stored uniquely, but it may fail to detect that two dotted-pairs are equal (i.e., consist of the same atoms within the same tree shape). This failure will occur when two such equal dotted-pairs occur in different list nodes in memory. On the other hand, if we wish to test for identical, shared, dotted-pairs, EQ will serve this purpose. For example, (EQ (CONS 1 2) (CONS 1 2)) may return NIL because the two dotted-pairs (1 . 2) and (1 . 2) may live in different list-area nodes, which are then represented by distinct typed-pointers.

© Gary D. Knott 2017
G. D. Knott, *Interpreting LISP*, DOI 10.1007/978-1-4842-2707-7_9

For (CAR x), v[CAR] receives a typed-pointer j to $v[x]$ as input. If $v[x]$ is not a dotted-pair, CAR is being used erroneously. Otherwise the typed-pointer $P_j.car$ is returned.

For (CDR x), v[CDR] receives a typed-pointer k to $v[x]$ as input. If $v[x]$ is not a dotted-pair, CDR is being used erroneously. Otherwise the typed-pointer $P_k.cdr$ is returned.

For (CONS $x\,y$), v[CONS] receives two typed-pointers as input: one typed-pointer j that points to $v[x]$ and one typed-pointer k that points to $v[y]$. An unoccupied list node P_h is obtained and $P_h.car$ is set to j and $P_h.cdr$ is set to k. Strictly, the types of the typed-pointers j and k must each be either 0 (dotted-pair), 8 (ordinary atom), or 9 (number atom). Then the typed-pointer $se(h)$ is returned. CONS is one of the few LISP functions that consumes memory. CONS requires that a new list node be allocated at each invocation.

For (SETQ $x\,y$), v[SETQ] receives two typed-pointers as input: one typed-pointer j that points to x and another typed-pointer k that points to y (remember SETQ is a special form). If j is positive or the value x pointed to by j is a number atom or a function or a special form, there is an error since x must be an ordinary atom. (Remember, the type-code field of a typed-pointer contains the sign-bit of the 32-bit computer word it is packed into.) If j is not positive and the value x pointed to by j is an ordinary atom, then $v[y]$ is computed by applying EVAL to the S-expression y whose typed-pointer is k. This results in a typed-pointer i that points to $v[y]$. Then the row determined by j in the atom table where the ordinary atom x resides has its value field set to the index corresponding to i and its typecode set to the type of $v[y]$, which is given in the typed-pointer i, except when $v[y]$ is an unnamed function or unnamed special form, in which case the occurrence of the typecode 14 or 15 for $v[y]$ results in the newly assigned value of x having, respectively, the typecode 12 or 13 instead.

Exercise 9.1: Specify an S-expression y such that $v[($SETQ A $y)] = v[($SETQ A (QUOTE $y))]$.

Solution 9.1: $y =$ NIL will suffice.

Exercise 9.2: What occurs when (SETQ X PLUS) is executed?

Solution 9.2: First, recall that we interpret v[PLUS] as a set of ordered pairs. Let's denote this set by {PLUS}. Then SETQ *redefines* the v meta-operator so that v[X] is now {PLUS}. Of course, within the LISP Interpreter program, {PLUS} is represented as a typed-pointer whose typecode is 10, and whose pointer part is some conventional value useful in identifying {PLUS}. After the SETQ application has been done, the row in the atom table where the ordinary atom X occurs has its type-field and value-field set to the typecode part and pointer part of this typed-pointer that represents {PLUS}.

Exercise 9.3: What is the set of ordered pairs denoted by {PLUS}?

Solution 9.3: $\{((a, b), a + b) \mid a \in R, b \in R\}$ where R denotes the set of real numbers.

Exercise 9.4: What is $v[$(CONS (SETQ B T) (EVAL (SETQ A (QUOTE B))))$]$?

Solution 9.4: (T . T), assuming the arguments of CONS are evaluated from left to right.

CHAPTER 10

■ ■ ■

List Notation

Some forms of nonatomic S-expressions arise so frequently there is a special notation for them. A dotted-pair of the form $(S_1 . (S_2 . (\cdots . (S_k . \text{NIL}) \cdots)))$ where $S_1, S_2, \ldots, S_k$ are all S-expressions is called a *list* and is written as $(S_1\ S_2\ \ldots\ S_k)$, which is the sequence of S-expressions $S_1, S_2, \ldots, S_k$ written with intervening blanks and enclosed in parentheses. There is no confusion with dot notation since there are no dots between the S_i elements in the list. There may, of course, be dots within some or all of the elements $S_1, \ldots, S_k$, but then they are necessarily enclosed in parentheses and the dots occur at lower levels. Any element S_i that qualifies may itself be written in either list notation or dotted-pair notation. But, remember, not every nonatomic S-expression is representable as a list.

The list (S_1) of the single element S_1 is written in dotted-pair notation as $(S_1 . \text{NIL})$. By analogy, the atom NIL is used to denote the list of no elements. The symbol pattern "()" is also used to denote the empty list; it is to be understood as a synonym for NIL.

> **Exercise 10.1:** Write the list (A B) in dot notation.
>
> **Solution 10.1:** (A . (B . NIL)).
>
> **Exercise 10.2:** How do we distinguish dots within ellipses from "true" dots used in dotted-pairs when writing text about S-expressions?
>
> **Exercise 10.3:** Write the S-expression (1 . (2 . (3 . NIL))) in list notation.
>
> **Solution 10.3:** (1 2 3).
>
> **Exercise 10.4:** Is every list a dotted-pair?
>
> **Solution 10.4:** All lists are dotted-pairs except the empty list, NIL. The empty list is represented by an atom.

© Gary D. Knott 2017

G. D. Knott, *Interpreting LISP*, DOI 10.1007/978-1-4842-2707-7_10

Exercise 10.5: Is every dotted-pair a list?

Solution 10.5: No. Only nonatomic S-expressions with a right-embedded NIL as shown above are lists. For example, (X . X) is not a list and neither is (NIL . 3).

Pictorially, a nonempty list $(S_1 \ldots S_k)$ is of the form:

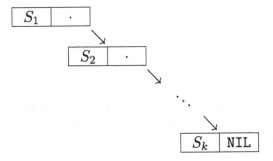

Exercise 10.6: What is the pictorial form and dot notation form of the 3 element list (NIL (T . T) X)?

Solution 10.6:

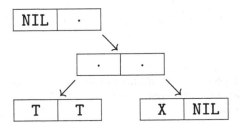

The dot-notation form is: (NIL . ((T . T) . (X . NIL))).

Exercise 10.7: How many final close parentheses occur together at the end of a k element list written in dot notation?

Solution 10.7: Exactly k final close parentheses occur.

Exercise 10.8: Is NIL a list of 0 elements?

Solution 10.8: NIL *represents* the empty list, but NIL *is* an ordinary atom. The class of lists consists of one atom, NIL, and an infinite number of certain nonatomic S-expressions.

Exercise 10.9: If s is a list and x is an S-expression, what is $z = v[(\text{CONS } x\ s)]$?

Solution 10.9: z is a list. Its first element is x and its remainder is the list s. Thus CONS can be used to construct a new list formed by adding an additional element at the head of a given list. In this example, the list s shares all its list nodes with the list z, which has an additional initial node. Such sharing of list nodes is common in S-expressions and is an elegant feature of LISP.

A list whose elements consist of atoms or lists, where these lists are recursively constrained in the same manner, is called a *pure list*. A pure list can be written entirely in list notation without dots appearing at any level.

Note that the notation used for specifying function application statements as LISP interpreter input is just list notation for certain S-expressions involving certain atoms! Thus almost every legal LISP input statement is an S-expression that is either an atom or a list, which itself has elements that are either atoms or lists. The only exception is that arguments to QUOTE can be arbitrary S-expressions. This is often summarized by saying that, in LISP, programs are data. Some data are programs too, but not every S-expression is legal LISP input. For any particular LISP interpreter, of course, there will be specific behaviors programmed in it that determine what happens for various illegal inputs.

Exercise 10.10: What is $v[(\text{EVAL } (\text{CONS } (\text{QUOTE CONS}) (\text{CONS } 2\ (\text{CONS } 3\ \text{NIL})))]$?

Solution 10.10: $(2\ .\ 3)$.

Exercise 10.11: What is $v[(\text{EVAL } (\text{QUOTE } (\text{CONS } (\text{QUOTE CAR}) (\text{QUOTE } (A\ .\ B))))]$?

Solution 10.11: The result is the same as

```
v[(EVAL . ((QUOTE
              . ((CONS . ((QUOTE . (CAR . NIL))
                          . ((QUOTE . ((A . B) . NIL)) . NIL)))
                 . NIL)) . NIL))]
  = (CAR . (A . B)).
```

Exercise 10.12: What is $v[(\text{T }\ .\ \text{NIL})]$?

Solution 10.12: Undefined. $v[\text{T}]$ is not a function or special form as is required for v to be defined on this form of input.

Remember that a function does not have to be designed to accept any member of the set of S-expressions as input. We have functions that only work on atoms or only on dotted-pairs, and a programmer can circumscribe the legal input in almost any manner desired. A function that is designed to work on a proper subset of S-expressions is called a *partial function* (in contrast to a *total function*). What happens when a partial function is called with one or more illegal input arguments is implementation dependent. Ideally, a partial function would be programmed to check its arguments and reject any illegal input with an accompanying error message. However, even when this is possible, it may sometimes be perceived to be too inefficient, and thus many built-in LISP functions and special forms may give nonsense results, loop, or crash when given illegal arguments. We summarize this by saying such functions and special forms are undefined on illegal input.

Now we may define the built-in function LIST. Unlike the previous functions and special forms we have seen, LIST may be invoked with differing numbers of arguments.

- LIST: **function with a varying number of arguments**

    $v[(\text{LIST } x_1\, x_2 \ldots x_k)] = v[(\text{CONS } x_1\, (\text{CONS } x_2\, (\text{CONS} \ldots (\text{CONS } x_k\, \text{NIL})) \ldots))].$

Exercise 10.13: What is $v[(\text{LIST NIL})]$? What is $v[(\text{LIST})]$?

Solution 10.13: $v[(\text{LIST NIL})] = (\text{NIL}) = (\text{NIL . NIL}).$
$v[(\text{LIST})]$ could consistently be defined to be NIL, but as we have defined the function LIST above, $v[(\text{LIST})]$ is undefined; $v[\text{LIST}]$ on the other hand is a built-in function. (Again, just because some input is undefined doesn't mean it is necessarily so for any particular LISP interpreter; to say some input is undefined means the LISP interpreter for this dialect has carte blanche as to its behavior.)

CHAPTER 11

■ ■ ■

More Special Forms

- AND: **special form with a varying number of arguments**

  $v[(\text{AND } x_1\, x_2 \ldots x_k)] = \text{if } v[x_1] \neq \text{NIL and } v[x_2] \neq \text{NIL and} \ldots$
  $v[x_k] \neq \text{NIL then T else NIL}.$

  The special form AND is evaluated using lazy evaluation; this means that the arguments are evaluated and tested against NIL from left to right and the first NIL-valued argument is the last argument evaluated.

- OR: **special form with a varying number of arguments**

  $v[(\text{OR } x_1\, x_2 \ldots x_k)] = \text{if } v[x_1] \neq \text{NIL or } v[x_2] \neq \text{NIL or} \ldots \text{or}$
  $v[x_k] \neq \text{NIL then T else NIL}.$

  The special form OR is evaluated using lazy evaluation; the arguments are evaluated and tested against NIL from left to right and the first non-NIL-valued argument is the last argument evaluated.

  Exercise 11.1: What should $v[(\text{AND})]$ and $v[(\text{OR})]$ be defined to be?

  Solution 11.1: One consistent choice is to define $v[(\text{AND})] = \text{T}$ and $v[(\text{OR})] = \text{NIL}$. This is somewhat analogous to the definition that an empty sum is 0 and an empty product is 1.

- COND: **special form with a varying number of arguments**

  $v[(\text{COND } (p_1\, q_1)\, (p_2\, q_2) \ldots (p_k\, q_k))] = \text{if } v[p_1] \neq \text{NIL then } v[q_1], \text{ else if }$
  $v[p_2] \neq \text{NIL then } v[q_2], \ldots, \text{else if } v[p_k] \neq \text{NIL then } v[q_k], \text{ else NIL}.$

  COND stands for *conditional*. It is the primary branching operator in LISP. Each argument to COND must be a two-element list whose elements are potentially evaluatable. The special form COND is

© Gary D. Knott 2017
G. D. Knott, *Interpreting LISP*, DOI 10.1007/978-1-4842-2707-7_11

evaluated using lazy evaluation; the length-two list arguments are examined from left to right and the first component of each is evaluated until the resulting value is not NIL, then the value of the associated second component is returned. Only as many p_i's as needed are evaluated, and at most one q_1 is evaluated. The special form COND is necessary both theoretically and practically. With COND, we can, in principle, dispense with AND and OR. Note:

$$v[(\text{AND } a \; b)] = v[(\text{COND } ((\text{EQ NIL } a) \text{ NIL}) ((\text{EQ NIL } b) \text{ NIL}) (\text{T T}))], \text{ and}$$

$$v[(\text{OR } a \; b)] = v[(\text{COND } ((\text{EQ } b \text{ NIL}) (\text{COND } ((\text{EQ } a \text{ NIL}) \text{ NIL}) (\text{T T}))) (\text{T T}))].$$

In [McC78], McCarthy writes: "I invented conditional expressions in connection with a set of chess legal move routines I wrote in FORTRAN for the IBM 704 at M.I.T. during 1957-58. This program did not use list processing. The IF statement provided in FORTRAN 1 and FORTRAN 2 was very awkward to use, and it was natural to invent a function XIF(M,N1,N2) whose value was N1 or N2 according to whether the expression M was zero or not. The function shortened many programs and made them easier to understand, but it had to be used sparingly, because all three arguments had to be evaluated before XIF was entered, since XIF was called as an ordinary FORTRAN function though written in machine language. This led to the invention of the true conditional expression which evaluates only one of N1 and N2 according to whether M is true or false and to a desire for a programming language that would allow its use."

Exercise 11.2: What is $v[(\text{OR (COND } ((\text{EQ NIL T}) \text{ NIL})$ $(\text{T NIL})) \text{ NIL})]$?

Solution 11.2: NIL.

Exercise 11.3: Do AND and OR require that arguments that evaluate to NIL or T be supplied?

Solution 11.3: No.

Exercise 11.4: What is $v[(\text{AND (COND } ((\text{SETQ A NIL}) \text{ T})$ $(\text{T T}) ((\text{SETQ A T}) \text{ T})) \text{ A (SETQ A } 0))]$?

Solution 11.4: NIL, and $v[\text{A}] = \text{NIL}$ afterward as a result of the assignment side-effect.

Exercise 11.5: Suppose A is an ordinary atom that has been assigned a number value with an application of SETQ. Write a LISP functional application command that causes the ceiling of the value of A to be printed out.

Solution 11.5: (COND ((EQ (FLOOR A) A) A) (T (PLUS 1 (FLOOR A)))).

Exercise 11.6: Suppose $v[S] = 1$. What is $v[((COND ((EQ NIL S) OR) (T AND)) S (NOT S))]$?

Exercise 11.7: What would be the effect if T were to be redefined so as to have the value 3 rather than itself?

Solution 11.7: The effect would be minor. But leaving T undefined would not be so benign. And redefining NIL to be 3 would seriously damage LISP.

You may have noticed that we have lapsed into the usual sloppiness found in discussions of programming languages (for good reason). We say "the special form COND is necessary ..." when we should say "the special form $v[COND]$, whose name is COND, is necessary ...". It is convenient to agree to tolerate such ambiguity.

CHAPTER 12

■ ■ ■

Defining Functions: λ-Expressions

We can use the LISP interpreter to compute the value of combinations of built-in functions and special forms applied to arguments, but to use LISP as a programming language rather than as a curious kind of calculator, we must have a way to *define* functions of our own choosing and use them, rather than just use unnamed compositions of preexisting functions.

The special form LAMBDA is used in LISP to *create* a user-defined function. LAMBDA takes two arguments, which are both S-expressions. The first argument is a list of ordinary atoms denoting the *formal arguments* of the function being defined, and the second argument is an S-expression expressing the definition of the function being defined. This second argument is required to be legal LISP input, so it is either an atom or a functional application expression. This second argument is called the *body* of the function being defined.

A list expressing an application of the special form LAMBDA is called a LISP λ-expression. For example, the λ-expression (LAMBDA (X Y) (CONS Y X)) denotes a function. That means, conceptually, its value is a set of ordered pairs. It is the function that, given two S-expressions, a and b, as input, returns the dotted-pair $(b . a)$ as output. Note this function has no name. In order to use this function in LISP, we can enter ((LAMBDA (X Y) (CONS Y X)) 2 3) into the LISP interpreter, and (3 . 2) will be printed out. In the λ-expression (LAMBDA (X Y) (CONS Y X)), the S-expression (CONS Y X) is the body and (X Y) is the *list of formal arguments*.

Continuing this example, the evaluation of ((LAMBDA (X Y) (CONS Y X)) 2 3) proceeds by *binding* the value of the first actual argument 2 to the first formal argument X, *binding* the value of the second actual argument 3 to the second formal argument Y, and then evaluating the body (CONS Y X) by computing $v[(\text{CONS Y X})]$ with the understanding that each occurrence of X in the body is evaluated to yield its associated bound value 2 and each occurrence of Y in the body is evaluated to yield its associated bound value 3. This means that $v[\text{X}] = 2$ and $v[\text{Y}] = 3$ in the body expression (CONS Y X), regardless of the global values of X and Y in the atom table.

Let a be a list of $k \geq 0$ ordinary atoms and let b be an evaluatable S-expression. In general, the value of the λ-expression (LAMBDA a b) is defined so that $v[(\text{LAMBDA } a\ b)]$ equals the function that is computed on a list of k actual arguments r by computing $e[b, a, r]$, where $e[b, a, r] = v[b]$ in the *context* such that $v[ai] = ri$ for $1 \leq i \leq k$. The symbol e stands

© Gary D. Knott 2017
G. D. Knott, *Interpreting LISP*, DOI 10.1007/978-1-4842-2707-7_12

for environmental evaluation. It is a form of the *v*-operator that depends upon a *context* specified by a binding of actual argument values to formal arguments.

It is awkward to write a λ-expression to specify a function for each use, so we adopt a device to give names to functions. The value of a λ-expression can be assigned a name using SETQ. Thus, for example, evaluating (SETQ G (LAMBDA (X Y) (CONS Y X))) results in the ordinary atom G having the value *v*[(LAMBDA (X Y) (CONS Y X))]. The result that is printed out is conventionally understood to be the set of ordered pairs conceptually assigned to G, which is *v*[(LAMBDA (X Y) (CONS Y X))], and this is denoted by "{user function: G}". Now we can write (G 2 3) to obtain (3 . 2).

If you look at various LISP dialects, you will find that a special form variously called DEFINE or DEFUN (meaning define-function) is commonly used to assign a function to be the value of an ordinary atom, but there is no reason SETQ can't serve this purpose, so we eschew DEFUN in this book. The use of DEFUN is often coupled with a mechanism for allowing an ordinary atom to have an S-expression value *and* a function value simultaneously. This option is not possible as we have defined the atom table and doesn't seem very felicitous in any event.

Note that the definition of SETQ is that the result is the value of its first argument *after* assignment. This means that the first argument already has a user-defined *named* function as its value, which appears as the result when SETQ is used to assign a function to an ordinary atom.

The most interesting case of defining and naming a function arises when recursion is utilized. For example:

```
(SETQ FACT (LAMBDA (X)
                (COND ((EQ X 0) 1)
                      (T (TIMES X (FACT (DIFFERENCE X 1)))))))
```

which defines the factorial function *fact* (*n*) = 1 2 ·3 ... ·(*n* − 1) *n*. This definition is an *impredicative* definition; that means the name FACT, which is being assigned a value, is itself used in defining that value. This is an uncomfortable state of affairs, but completely understandable pragmatically.

What the special form LAMBDA really does is CONS its two arguments together and returns an unnamed-function-typed-pointer to the resulting dotted-pair; this is a typed-pointer whose typecode is 14. The arguments themselves are not examined until the function is actually applied. If this unnamed function that is represented as a dotted-pair is assigned as the value of an ordinary atom *b*, the value of *b* is then just the pointer to the dotted-pair, and the type of this value is set to 12 to indicate a user-defined function. Thus, for example, when FACT as assigned above is used, the recursive reference to FACT within the body is correctly interpreted because the value of FACT *at the time of evaluation of the body* is consistently defined.

Remember that *v*[(SETQ *x y*)] has been defined to be *v*[*x*] *after* *v*[*x*] is made equal to *v*[*y*]; but when *y* is a λ-expression, this does not hold. In this case, *v*[*y*] is a typed-pointer to the CONSed dotted-pair representing the value of the λ-expression *y*. The typecode of this typed-pointer is 14. However, after the assignment to redefine *v*[*x*], *v*[*x*] is a typed-pointer to the same dotted-pair, but the typecode of *v*[*x*] is 12 rather than 14. Thus in the case of assigning the value of a λ-expression *y* to an ordinary atom *x*, the typecode of *v*[*x*] after the assignment is *not* the typecode of *v*[*y*]. This awkward exception arises because functions need not have names. If names were always required, this distinction encoded in typecode values would be unnecessary.

Exercise 12.1: What is $v[((\text{LAMBDA} (X) X) y)]$?

Solution 12.1: $v[y]$. So typing $((\text{LAMBDA} (X) X) y)$ produces the same result as typing y.

Exercise 12.2: What does (SETQ CONS (LAMBDA (X) (CONS 1 X))) do?

Solution 12.2: The function CONS is redefined to be a nonterminating recursive function. The CONS in the body refers to the same atom as the atom being reassigned a value, and in the future, as at all other times, that atom has just one value. Most versions of LISP do not permit atoms whose values are built-in functions or special forms to be redefined in this manner.

Exercise 12.3: (J. McCarthy) Specify an input non-atomic S-expression, a, which has itself as its value.

Solution 12.3: a = ((LAMBDA (X) (LIST X (LIST (QUOTE QUOTE) X))).
(QUOTE (LAMBDA (X) (LIST X (LIST (QUOTE QUOTE) X)))))

Exercise 12.4: Is (LAMBDA NIL 3.1415926) a legal λ-expression?

Solution 12.4: Yes. A function with no arguments is a *constant*. If it is not a constant, it is not a function, rather it is a pseudofunction, such as a random-number generator.

The name LAMBDA and the term λ-expression are borrowed from the so-called λ-calculus of Alonzo Church [Kle52]. This is a mathematical invention used to explore the syntactic and semantic nature and power of substitution. It is, in some sense, a theory of macro languages.

CHAPTER 13

■ ■ ■

More Functions

There are many built-in functions in LISP that are not logically required to be built in.
They are there for convenience, and in some cases because they are faster that way. The
three functions presented below are built-in functions that have definitions in terms of
other more basic functions and special forms.

- APPEND: **function**

    Defined by:

```
(SETQ APPEND
      (LAMBDA (X Y)
              (COND ((EQ X NIL) Y)
                    ((ATOM X) (CONS X Y))
                    (T (CONS (CAR X) (APPEND (CDR X) Y))))))
```

This version of APPEND is slightly more general than the commonly found definition,
which omits the ((ATOM X) (CONS X Y)) pair. Given two *lists* $(a_1 a_2 \ldots a_h)$ and $(b_1 b_2 \ldots b_k)$ as
input, the list $(a_1 a_2 \ldots a_h b_1 b_2 \ldots b_k)$ is produced as the output. The input is not damaged in
any way. In a sense, this function embodies the essence of LISP. When you understand in
detail at the machine level what happens during the application of this function to arguments,
then you will understand the essence of LISP.

For example, with $v[A] = (1\ A\ 2)$, $v[(APPEND\ A\ (LIST\ 7))] = (1\ A\ 2\ 7)$, and $v[(APPEND$
$A\ 7)] = (1\ .\ (A\ .\ (2\ .\ 7)))$; APPEND joins two lists; its action on atoms is more
arbitrary.

Note APPEND adds to the end of a list and CONS adds to the front of a list. These
functions are asymmetric, however; CONS can add only one element at a time to the front
of a list, while APPEND can add an entire list of elements to a list at its end. Also CONS is
efficient, while APPEND is inefficient; this is because a linked list with a pointer to the first
element is an insufficient data structure for allowing direct access to the end of the list.
(We could use other data structures such as doubly linked [bidirectionally linked] binary
trees or hash tables instead of singly linked lists [Knu68, Knu73], and indeed this has been
done in some implementations of LISP.)

© Gary D. Knott 2017
G. D. Knott, *Interpreting LISP*, DOI 10.1007/978-1-4842-2707-7_13

Exercise 13.1: What is $v[$(APPEND (QUOTE (A . NIL)) T)]? What is $v[$(APPEND (QUOTE (A B)) NIL)]? What is $v[$(APPEND T T)]?

Exercise 13.2: Suppose the ordinary atom X has the value (NIL . (T . NIL)) and that the ordinary atom Y has the value (X . (Y . NIL)), where these S-expressions are stored in the list area as follows:

atom table					list area	
	name	type	value		1	$(-1, 3)$
1	NIL	8	1	–	2	$(-3, 4)$
2	T	8	2	–	3	$(-2, -1)$
3	X	0	1	–	4	$(-4, -1)$
4	Y	0	2	–	5	first free

Assume new list area nodes are allocated and used in the order 5, 6, ... , etc. Tabulate the changes that occur in the list area when (APPEND X Y) is executed, and present the resulting contents of the list area. (Actually, the typed-pointer value denoted by –1 is $oa(1) = 1000 :: 1$.) What exactly is the typed-pointer denoted by –3?

Exercise 13.3: Write a version of APPEND that joins the two input lists when both arguments are lists, and adds the second argument as the last *list* member of the first argument when the first argument is a list and the second argument is an atom.

- REVERSE: **function**

Defined by:

```
(SETQ REVERSE
      (LAMBDA (X)
              (COND ((ATOM X) X)
                    (T (APPEND (REVERSE (CDR X)) (CONS (CAR X) NIL)))))))
```

Exercise 13.4: Suppose the functions A and B are defined by:

```
(SETQ A (LAMBDA (X Y)
               (COND ((EQ X NIL) Y)
                     (T (B (REVERSE X) Y)))))
```

and

```
(SETQ B (LAMBDA (X Y)
                (COND ((EQ X NIL) Y)
                      (T (B (CDR X) (CONS (CAR X) Y)))))))
```

What does A do?

Solution 13.4: The function A is another version of APPEND. It behaves the same way APPEND does on list arguments.

● EQUAL: **predicate**

Defined by:

```
(SETQ EQUAL (LAMBDA (X Y)
                    (COND ((OR (ATOM X) (ATOM Y)) (EQ X Y))
                          ((EQUAL (CAR X) (CAR Y)) (EQUAL (CDR X) (CDR Y)))
                          (T NIL))))
```

Unlike the EQ predicate, EQUAL is guaranteed to return T for equal S-expressions and NIL for unequal S-expressions.

Exercise 13.5: Is the last (T NIL) pair appearing in the definition of EQUAL necessary?

Solution 13.5: No, as we have defined COND herein it is not necessary, but it is harmless, and it is required in some dialects of LISP where a COND does not have a NIL final value by default.

Exercise 13.6: Does the EQUAL predicate consume list area nodes during its application?

Solution 13.6: No. The CONS function is not applied directly or indirectly.

Exercise 13.7: Define a LISP function LENGTH, which takes a list as input and returns the number of elements in the list as output.

Exercise 13.8: Define a LISP predicate LISTP, which returns T if its assignment is a list and returns NIL otherwise.

Solution 13.8: Define LISTP by:

```
(SETQ LISTP (LAMBDA (S) (COND ((ATOM S) (EQ S NIL))
                              (T (LISTP (CDR S))))))
```

49

Exercise 13.9: Define a LISP predicate MEMBER, which returns T if the input S-expression, *a*, is an element of the input list, *s*, and which returns NIL otherwise.

Solution 13.9: Define MEMBER by:

```
(SETQ MEMBER (LAMBDA (A S)
                (COND ((EQ S NIL) NIL)
                      ((EQUAL A (CAR S)) T)
                      (T (MEMBER A (CDR S)))))))
```

Exercise 13.10: Define a LISP function PLACE, which is like MEMBER in that an input list *s* is searched for an S-expression *a*, but the remainder of the list *s* after the point at which *a* is found is returned as the result, or the atom NULL is returned as the result if *a* is not an element of *s*. Why is NULL specified as the atom that is returned to indicate a failure?

Exercise 13.11: Define a LISP predicate DEEPMEM, which returns T if the input S-expression *a* occurs as an element of the input list *s*, or as an element of any sublist of *s* at any level, and returns NIL otherwise. You may assume that *s* is a pure list, all of whose elements are atoms or pure lists.

Solution 13.11: Define DEEPMEM by:

```
(SETQ DEEPMEM (LAMBDA (A S)
                  (COND ((ATOM S) NIL)
                        ((OR (EQUAL A (CAR S)) (DEEPMEM A (CAR S))) T)
                        (T (DEEPMEM A (CDR S)))))))
```

Exercise 13.12: Define a LISP function TRUNC, which takes a non-empty list *s* as input and returns a list identical to *s*, but with the last element removed.

Exercise 13.13: Define a LISP function DEPTH, which takes an S-expression *a* as input and returns 0 if *a* is an atom and returns the number of levels in the binary tree picture of *a* otherwise. Thus the depth of the S-expression *a* is the maximum number of parentheses pairs which enclose an atom in *a*.

Exercise 13.14: What happens when ((SETQ G (LAMBDA (X) (CONS X (G X)))) 3) is typed in to the LISP interpreter?

Solution 13.14: First, the value of the ordinary atom G will become the specified function, and then the LISP interpreter will run out of stack space because of the infinite recursion specified in G applied to 3. Note that the list area will not be exhausted, since no CONS application is ever actually consummated.

Exercise 13.15: Define a *flat* list to be a list whose elements are atoms. Write a LISP function FLATP to test whether an S-expression is flat. Write another LISP function FLAT that returns a flat list containing all the atoms found within the input S-expression x.

Exercise 13.16: Define a LISP predicate PURE, which takes an S-expression x as input and returns T if x is a pure list and returns NIL otherwise.

Exercise 13.17: Can there be two list area entries P_i and P_j with $i \neq j$ such that $P_i = P_j$? That is, does list-node sharing preclude duplicate list-nodes existing?

Solution 13.17: Yes, duplicate list-nodes can exist. But it is interesting to contemplate ways in which duplicate list-nodes can be avoided.

CHAPTER 14

■ ■ ■

Defining Special Forms

User-defined special forms are created by applying the special form SPECIAL, which is completely analogous to the special form LAMBDA, except that an unnamed-special-form-typed-pointer to the dotted-pair of the input arguments is returned, so that the result will, upon later use, be interpreted as a special form rather than a function. An unnamed-special-form-typed-pointer has the typecode 15.

Thus the body and formal argument list of a special form created by SPECIAL are represented by CONSing the input arguments together to form a dotted-pair and an unnamed-special-form-typed-pointer whose pointer part indexes this dotted-pair is returned. Just as with λ-expressions, the typecode of the value of an ordinary atom that is assigned an unnamed-special-form is forced to be 13 rather than 15. The value 13 is the typecode denoting a named special form. The newly reset value field contains a pointer to the dotted-pair of the argument list and body of the special form.

Let a be a list of $k \geq 0$ ordinary atoms and let b be an evaluatable S-expression. In general, the value of the special form-expression (SPECIAL a b) is defined as $v[$(SPECIAL a b)$]$, which equals the function that is computed on a list of k actual arguments r by computing $e[b, a, r]$, where $e[b, a, r] = v[b]$ in the context such that $v[a_i] = r_i$ for $1 \leq i \leq k$. Unlike a λ-expression, the actual arguments r are taken as they are given and are not computed by evaluating the given actual arguments.

It is important to note that the definition of the value (i.e., the meaning) of a LISP special form or function in terms of a context is *not* the same as the meaning that is induced using the often-used *substitution* rule in Algol, where we would say that $v[$(SPECIAL a b)$]$ is that function which is computed on a list of k actual arguments r by computing the value of b with r_i substituted for each occurrence of a_i in b for $1 \leq i \leq k$. Binding temporarily supersedes the meanings of symbols in the atom table, as seen by every ordinary atom evaluation that is done while the binding is in force, whereas substitution does not cover up such meanings everywhere.

For example, (SETQ EVALQUOTE (SPECIAL (X) (EVAL X))) defines the special form EVALQUOTE, which is used in the following exercise.

© Gary D. Knott 2017
G. D. Knott, *Interpreting LISP*, DOI 10.1007/978-1-4842-2707-7_14

Exercise 14.1: Suppose the atom A has the undefined value. What output results from the following commands given in sequence?

```
(SETQ B (QUOTE A))
(EVALQUOTE B)
(EVAL (QUOTE B))
(EVAL B)
```

Solution 14.1: The four successive outputs that result are: (1) A, (2) A, (3) A, and (4) undefined.

Exercise 14.2: Suppose the atom X has the undefined value. Keep in mind that EVALQUOTE is defined with a formal argument X. What output results from the following commands given in sequence?

```
(EVALQUOTE X)
(SETQ X 3)
(EVAL (QUOTE X))
(EVALQUOTE X)
```

Solution 14.2: The four successive outputs that result are: (1) X, (2) 3, (3) 3, and (4) X.

Exercise 14.3: Define the special form SETQQ, which assigns the value of its unevaluated second argument to its first atom-valued unevaluated argument so as to become the value of the first atom.

Solution 14.3: This would be defined as:

```
(SETQ SETQQ
      (SPECIAL (X Y)
               (EVAL (CONS (QUOTE SETQ)
                           (CONS X (CONS (CONS (QUOTE QUOTE)
                                               (CONS Y NIL))
                                   NIL))))))
```

This special form operates so that the name bound to X is used independently of any context. Thus, for example, (SETQQ P Q) sets the current value of the atom P equal to the atom Q in any context, in or out of a function body or special form body. However, this current value is lost when the context in which P has been assigned a bound value terminates.

Exercise 14.4: Define the function SET, which assigns its evaluated second argument to become the value of its atom-valued evaluated first argument.

Solution 14.4: This is defined by:

```
(SETQ SET (LAMBDA (X Y)
                 (EVAL (CONS (QUOTE SETQ)
                            (CONS X (CONS (QUOTE Y) NIL))))))
```

Another solution is:

```
(SETQ SET (SPECIAL (X Y)
                 (EVAL (CONS (QUOTE SETQ)
                            (CONS (EVAL X) (CONS Y NIL))))))
```

Exercise 14.5: SETQ stands for set-quote; explain how the special form QUOTE is related to SETQ.

Because of the possibly counterintuitive behavior of some functions or special forms when applied to arguments whose names are also used as formal argument names, where the substitution rule and the binding rule give differing results, such functions and special forms should be used sparingly. It is a good idea to have useful functions and special forms like SET and EVALQUOTE *built in* to the LISP interpreter so that no such formal argument name conflicts can arise.

User-defined and unnamed functions and special forms are stored as simple dotted-pair S-expressions formed from the S-expressions given to define them. It is sometimes useful to explicitly look at the defining dotted-pair of a user-defined or unnamed function or special form. This can be done with the function BODY, defined as follows.

- BODY: **function**

  $v[(\text{BODY } x)]$ equals the dotted-pair, which encodes the definition of the user-defined or unnamed function or special form $v[x]$, such that CAR applied to the result is the formal argument list of x, and CDR applied to the result is the S-expression defining the body of x.

Exercise 14.6: What output will appear as the result of the following input?

```
(SETQ E (LAMBDA (X) (MINUS X)))
(BODY E)
```

Solution 14.6: {user-defined function: E} and ((X) MINUS X). (Remember ((X) . (MINUS X)) is ((X) MINUS X) in list-notation.)

Exercise 14.7: Define the special form IF such that:
$v[(\text{IF } a\ b\ c)] = \text{if } v[a] = \text{NIL then } v[c] \text{ else } v[b].$

Solution 14.7:

```
(SETQ IF (SPECIAL (A B C)
                  (COND ((EVAL A) (EVAL B))
                        (T (EVAL C)))))
```

CHAPTER 15

The Label Special Form

Recursive functions or special forms can be named and defined in LISP using SETQ. This is convenient, and we almost always define functions and special forms this way in practice. But this leaves a theoretical difficulty about the LAMBDA operator, namely, we *must* use SETQ and assign a name in order to define a recursive function. Thus not every desired function can, in theory, be written in place as a λ-expression. In order to dispose of this difficulty, the special form LABEL is introduced.

- LABEL: **special form**

  $v[(\text{LABEL } g\, h\, a_1 \dots a_k)] = e[(h\, v[a_1] \dots v[a_k]), g, h]$, where g is an ordinary atom and h is a λ-expression and $a_1, \dots, a_k$ are S-expressions. The idea is that $(\text{LABEL } g\, h\, a_1 \dots a_k) = v[(h\, a_1 \dots a_k)]$ in the context where the atom g is evaluated as the λ-expression h at every occurrence of g in the body of the λ-expression h. Thus g is, in effect, the name or label of h in the body of h during this evaluation of h on the supplied arguments $a_1, \dots, a_k$.

The extension of the definition of LABEL to apply to special forms is left as an exercise, since LABEL is primarily needed to provide a pleasant theoretical closure and is not often used in practice and, except for QUOTE, special forms are, in theory, avoidable by using QUOTE to protect the arguments of corresponding λ-expressions. Indeed, LABEL is not included in the LISP interpreter given below.

Exercise 15.1: Explain the following:

```
v[(LABEL FACTL
          (LAMBDA (X) (COND ((EQ X 0) 1)
                            (T (TIMES X (FACTL (DIFFERENCE X 1))))))
          3)]?
```

Exercise 15.2: Carefully state the appropriate definition of $(\text{LABEL } g\, h\, a_1 \dots a_k)$ where g is an ordinary atom and h is a special-form expression.

© Gary D. Knott 2017
G. D. Knott, *Interpreting LISP*, DOI 10.1007/978-1-4842-2707-7_15

CHAPTER 16

The Quote Macro

The special form QUOTE is used so frequently that a special notation is provided. The single quote or apostrophe symbol is used to denote a unary prefix operator, defined so that '*e* = (QUOTE *e*). Thus for example, the SET function can be defined by the input:

```
(SETQ SET (LAMBDA (X Y)
                  (EVAL (CONS 'SETQ (CONS X (CONS 'Y NIL)))))))
```

The single quote symbol acts as a macro; it is expanded upon input. Thus ' cannot be manipulated as an atom within LISP functions. Remember ' does not mean QUOTE standing alone; it must take an argument.

> **Exercise 16.1:** Can the expression "(QUOTE *e*) be written as "*e*?
>
> **Solution 16.1:** Yes.
>
> **Exercise 16.2:** Describe the objects *x* which satisfy $v['x] = v[x]$.
>
> **Solution 16.2:** $\{ x \mid v['x] = v[x] \} = \{ y \mid v[y] = y \}$, which is the set of all number atoms, LISP functions, LISP special forms, and certain non-atomic S-expressions that evaluate to themselves.
>
> **Exercise 16.3:** What is the history of the term *macro*?

© Gary D. Knott 2017

G. D. Knott, *Interpreting LISP*, DOI 10.1007/978-1-4842-2707-7_16

CHAPTER 17

■ ■ ■

More Functions

- NOT: **predicate**

  Defined by: (SETQ NOT (LAMBDA (X) (EQ X NIL))).

- NULL: **predicate**

  Defined by: (SETQ NULL (LAMBDA (X) (NOT X))).

  Note NULL is just a synonym for NOT. We may prefer to use NULL when testing for NIL and to use NOT when performing the Boolean operation of logical negation.

  Exercise 17.1: Show that $v[(\text{NOT } (\text{NULL } y))] = v[(\text{AND } y)]$.

- GREATERP: **predicate**

  $v[(\text{GREATERP } n\ m)] = $ if $v[n] > v[m]$ then T else NIL. $v[n]$ and $v[m]$ must be numbers.

- LESSP: **predicate**

  $v[(\text{LESSP } n\ m)] = $ if $v[n] < v[m]$ then T else NIL. $v[n]$ and $v[m]$ must be numbers.

  Exercise 17.2: Show that when x and y are integers in the following:

  v[(GREATERP x y)] = v[((LAMBDA (X Y) (GCHECK (DIFFERENCE (DIFFERENCE X Y) 1),
                                                      (DIFFERENCE Y X))) x y)]

© Gary D. Knott 2017
G. D. Knott, *Interpreting LISP*, DOI 10.1007/978-1-4842-2707-7_17

where GCHECK is defined by

```
(SETQ GCHECK (LAMBDA (A B)
                     (COND ((EQ A 0) T)
                           ((EQ B 0) NIL)
                           (T (GCHECK (PLUS A -1) (PLUS B -1)))))))
```

Exercise 17.3: Define the function GCD in LISP, where
$v[($GCD a $b$$)]$ is the greatest common positive integer divisor
of the two positive integers a and b. Hint: investigate the
Euclidean algorithm.

CHAPTER 18

■ ■ ■

More About Typed-Pointers

In order to handle number atoms efficiently as values within the LISP interpreter, we have used pointers to numbers in sketching the working of the v operator. This use of pointers is also required to allow functions to be treated as values. The guiding idea is that the LISP interpreter needs to know, at least potentially, the name or lexical expression associated with any value being manipulated, and every such value is represented by a typed-pointer to some complete representation of that value.

In particular, then, a number must be represented in a way that permits the proper result when printing it, using it as an argument in a computation or as a CONS argument, and when creating a new number as an intermediate result.

Consider:

```
v[3.1],
v[A], where v[A] has been made equal to 3 via (SETQ A 3),
v[(PLUS 2 3)],
v[(PLUS 2 A)],
v[(CONS (PLUS 2 A) 1)].
```

Whenever a number is computationally created, by evaluating (PLUS 2 3), for example, that number is entered in an available row in the number table, if and only if it is not already present. For such computationally created numbers, some time can be saved by *not* constructing the number-name text-string; in fact, for the sake of uniformity, we discard the text-string name of input numbers. Such nameless number atoms are called *lazy* number atoms. If a lazy number atom must be printed out, only then do we construct its text-string name. Also, the computationally-created number atoms that are no longer needed should, from time to time, be removed from the number table.

Similarly, a function or special form must be represented in a way which permits the proper result when applying it, printing it, or using it as an argument in a computation.

Consider:

```
v[PLUS],
v[(PLUS 2 3)],
v[(EVAL (APPEND 'PLUS '(2 3)))],
v[(EVAL (APPEND PLUS '(2 3)))].
```

© Gary D. Knott 2017
G. D. Knott, *Interpreting LISP*, DOI 10.1007/978-1-4842-2707-7_18

An appropriate internal representation of a function such as $v[\text{PLUS}]$ is as a typed-pointer to the atom PLUS, where this typed-pointer has the typecode 10, as opposed to 8, indicating that it refers to a built-in function, which is the value of the pointed-to atom. In this way, we know both the function and its name.

Thus, a built-in function that is the value of an ordinary atom x stored at an entry j in the atom table is represented by the typed-pointer $bf(j)$. This atom table entry appears as $[x, 10, t, -, -]$. The value field entry t is an integer that indicates the particular built-in function, which is the value of x. In contrast, the ordinary atom x is represented by the typed-pointer $oa(j)$.

Also, a built-in special form, which is the value of an ordinary atom x stored at an entry j in the atom table, is represented by the typed-pointer $bs(j)$. This atom table entry appears as $[x, 11, t, -, -]$. The value field entry t is an integer that indicates the particular built-in special form, which is the value of x.

A user-defined function is constructed by the special form LAMBDA by CONSing together the argument list and body S-expressions given as input and returning a typed-pointer to this constructed S-expression in the list area. This typed-pointer has the typecode 14, indicating an *unnamed function*. Similarly, the special form SPECIAL constructs a dotted-pair and returns a typed-pointer to this dotted-pair with the typecode 15, indicating an *unnamed special form*.

When SETQ assigns an unnamed function or special form to an ordinary atom, the value of that atom is henceforth represented by a typed-pointer to that atom whose typecode is 12 for a user-defined function and 13 for a user-defined special form. Suppose the ordinary atom F occupies row i in the atom table and suppose we evaluate (SETQ F (LAMBDA (X) 1)). Then the ordinary atom F has i : $[\text{F}, 12, j, -, -]$ as its row in the atom table, where $P_j = \boxed{\begin{array}{c|c} k & 1 \end{array}}$ and $P_k = \boxed{\begin{array}{c|c} \text{X} & \text{NIL} \end{array}}$. The typed-pointer representing $v[\text{F}]$ then has 12 as its typecode and i as its pointer part. This allows us to know the name as well as the defining S-expression of the function, which is the value of F.

> **Exercise 18.1:** Can the built-in function EQ be used to test whether two functions are equal?
>
> **Solution 18.1:** Two typed-pointers can be checked for equality with EQ, and thus EQ can be used to determine when exactly the same named identical built-in or user-defined function or special forms are presented. Identically defined user-defined functions or special forms that have different names (or different defining dotted-pairs if they are unnamed) cannot be successfully tested for equality with EQ. Of course, the general logical problem of deciding when two functions specified by formulas are the same is undecidable, although many special cases can be handled.

Exercise 18.2: How could two unnamed functions with the same shared defining dotted-pair be presented to EQ for comparison?

Solution 18.2: The rather pointless function (LAMBDA (X) (EQ X X)) allows the same defining dotted-pair, or indeed, the same typed-pointer to any value to be presented to EQ for comparison.

We may describe the typed-pointers used to represent built-in or user-defined named functions and special forms as *doubly indirect* typed-pointers. Of course the LISP interpreter must convert such a doubly indirect typed-pointer to the desired singly indirect index value whenever this is required.

CHAPTER 19

■ ■ ■

Binding Actual Values to Formal Arguments

In order to implement the e operator for evaluating λ-expression bodies within the LISP interpreter, we must devise a mechanistic way to bind actual arguments to formal arguments and to honor the contexts thus established during the time that a related λ-expression is being evaluated. There are several ways to do this. The earliest approach, which was employed in the original LISP interpreter for the IBM 704 and 709, was to maintain a so-called *association list*. It is convenient to describe this approach and then use it as a model to explain how a LISP interpreter works in effect, if not in fact.

The association list is a LISP list that is the value of the built-in ordinary atom ALIST. The elements of the association list are dotted-pairs $(n_i . v_i)$, where n_i is an ordinary atom used as a formal argument, and v_i is an S-expression or function, which is an actual argument bound to n_i. Such dotted-pairs are put on the association list as follows when a function call expression $(g\, a_1 \ldots a_k)$ is to be evaluated. The formal argument list of $v[g]$, $(f_1, \ldots, f_k)$ is retrieved and the formal argument—actual argument dotted-pairs $(f_i . v[a_i])$ (when $v[g]$ is a function), or $(f_i . a_i)$ (when $v[g]$ is a special form) are formed and CONSed onto $v[\text{ALIST}]$ in order from the first to the last argument. An exception is made within the LISP interpreter so that functions and special forms like $v[\text{PLUS}]$ are allowed to be elements in association list dotted-pairs. This is required since LISP functions and special forms may take functions and/or special forms as arguments.

Now the body of $v[g]$ is obtained and the LISP interpreter is *recursively* invoked to evaluate it. During this evaluation, whenever an ordinary atom d is encountered. It is evaluated in the current context by first searching the association list from front to back for the first dotted-pair of the form $(d . w)$; if such a pair is found, the value of d is taken to be w. Otherwise, if no such pair is found on $v[\text{ALIST}]$, then the value of d is sought in the atom table entry for d. When the body of $v[g]$ has been evaluated within the context given by the current association list, the initial k dotted-pairs corresponding to the formal argument bindings of $v[g]$ are removed from the association list $v[\text{ALIST}]$. This model of resolving the value bound to an ordinary atom is called *dynamic scoping*, as opposed to the *lexical* or *static* scoping found in languages like Algol.

In Algol, function definitions may be lexically nested in the defining text. The value of a variable x in the body of a function p is determined as the value bound to x in the closest function body in which the function p is nested, including the body of p itself in the case where x is a locally defined variable or an argument of p, or in the atom table if p is not

© Gary D. Knott 2017
G. D. Knott, *Interpreting LISP*, DOI 10.1007/978-1-4842-2707-7_19

nested within any other functions. This lexical scoping search to determine the value of a variable is equivalent to lexically substituting the actual value to be bound to x at the time of calling a function p, which has an formal argument named x for the name x within the function body of p, excepting those function bodies nested within p, which have a formal argument called x.

Suppose we have two functions, $f(a, b)$ and $g(b, c)$, at the same lexical level, where g is called from within f. With Algol lexical scoping, the value of a within g is the global atom table value of a, whether or not g is running called from f. With LISP dynamic scoping, the value of a within g is the global atom table value if g is running from a top-level call to g, and the value of a is the actual argument value passed to f for binding to a if g is running called from f. (Algol has its own complexities, in particular, Algol has some gnarly implications of its lexical static scoping binding rule. This is only a problem when procedures are declared nested within procedures and mixes the names of formal arguments and nonlocal variables; C avoids these problems by forbidding the declaration of lexically-nested procedures.)

Notice that if the same ordinary atom x is used several times in differing λ-expressions as a formal argument, and if the corresponding functions are called one within another, then the same atom x will occur several times in dotted-pairs on the association list during a certain time period. Whenever x must be evaluated, the latest existing binding will be used. This is exactly the right thing to do, but apparent mistakes can occur when this fact is forgotten.

For example, if we type in:

```
(SETQ G 3)                        followed by
(SETQ F (LAMBDA (X) (CONS X G)))   and
(SETQ B (LAMBDA (G X) (CONS G (F (PLUS X 1)))))
```

then $v[(B\ 2\ 0)] = (2\ .\ (1\ .\ 2))$, but $v[(F\ 1)] = (1\ .\ 3)$. The ordinary atom G occurring in the body of the function $v[F]$ is said to be a *free variable* of the function $v[F]$. In general, *any* ordinary atom occurring in a function or special form body that is not listed as a formal argument of that function or special form is a free variable of that function or special form.

When the body of a function or special form is evaluated in a context provided by the bound pairs of the association list, the values of the free variables encountered are determined by the current association list if possible. Thus you cannot write a function like $v[F]$ and expect its free variables to have the values of the atom table entries of those names, unless you are careful to not use those names elsewhere as formal arguments, or at least arrange to never have any of them bound on the association list when the function is called.

This situation is not so bad. We only have to use sufficient discipline to avoid picking formal argument names and global atom table names from among the same candidates whenever confusion might result.

A countervailing benefit of the simple LISP argument binding rule is that we can use the fact that the latest binding on the association list is the current value of an ordinary atom to skip passing arguments to functions explicitly when we know that the desired binding will already be in force. For example, consider:

```
(SETQ MAXF (LAMBDA (L F)
                (COND ((NULL (CDR L)) (CAR L))
                      (T (MH (CAR L) (MAXF (CDR L) F))))))
```

and

```
(SETQ MH (LAMBDA (A B)
                (COND ((GREATERP (F A) (F B)) A)
                      (T B)))).
```

Here F is a free variable in MH, which will be properly interpreted as the function bound to F when MAXF is invoked, since MH is only intended to be used from within MAXF. This device is called *skip-binding*.

There are situations, however, in which the evaluation of an apparently free variable done by following the simple association list model for context evaluation is clearly counterintuitive. Consider the example:

```
(SETQ F (LAMBDA (A)
               (G (PLUS A 1)
                  (LAMBDA (X) (CONS X A))))).
```

Here we have a function body consisting of a call to some function G, which is passed a function created by LAMBDA as one of its actual arguments, namely $v[(\text{LAMBDA (X) (CONS X A)})]$. The ordinary atom A is a free variable of this argument function, but A is a formal argument, not a free variable, of the containing function F being defined.

Now suppose we define G with (SETQ G (LAMBDA (A H) (H A))). Then $v[(\text{F } 1)] = (2 . 2)$. But, if we define G with (SETQ G (LAMBDA (O H) (H O))), then $v[(\text{F } 1)] = (2 . 1)$. Thus, in order to avoid such surprises, we have to not only avoid conflicts with our choice of global names and formal argument names, but we also must be aware of conflicts if we use the same names for formal arguments in different functions whenever functional arguments are used. This difficulty is called the *functional argument* problem or "funarg" problem.

> **Exercise 19.1:** Show that the functional argument difficulty can occur in the form of a free-variable conflict, without the use of a λ-expression or special-expression appearing as an actual argument.
>
> **Solution 19.1:** Consider:
>
> ```
> (SETQ Z (LAMBDA (X) (CONS X A)))
> (SETQ F (LAMBDA (A) (G (PLUS A 1) Z)))
> (SETQ G (LAMBDA (A H) (H A))).
> ```
>
> Then $v[(\text{F } 1)] = (2 . 2)$.

The functional argument problem is really just a matter of potentially misunderstanding *binding times*. A variable may be a global variable some times and a formal argument at other times during the evaluation of various S-expressions that are being evaluated in order to evaluate a root S-expression. The notion of free variable is syntactic; a variable is free with respect to a function or special form according to its appearance in the associated body; it is not a temporal notion. However, such function body S-expressions are evaluated in a temporal sequence, and particular variables may be assigned values (i.e., be *bound*) differently at different times. Every ordinary atom must have something bound to it whenever it is evaluated (or else we have an evaluation error), but at some times this value is found in the association list, and at other times it is found in the atom table. In any event, the value of an ordinary atom at a given point in time is that value to which it has been most recently bound. Thus the value of an ordinary atom may change with time. The time at which each temporal act of the binding of values to ordinary atom variables occurs is *as late as possible* in LISP.

Returning to the example above: consider $v[(F\ 1)]$, based on F defined by:

```
(SETQ F (LAMBDA (A)
            (G (PLUS A 1)
               (LAMBDA (X) (CONS X A)))))),
```

and G defined by (SETQ G (LAMBDA (A H) (H A))). We see that the value of A in (PLUS A 1) is 1 when (PLUS A 1) is evaluated, and this binding is found in the association list. But the value of A in (CONS X A) is 2 *when it is evaluated* and this later binding of 2 to A supersedes the earlier binding of A in the association list.

Late-as-possible binding is effected if binding occurs when functions are called; thus we will refer to this kind of binding as *call-time* binding, since the context that is used when a formal argument of a function or special form is evaluated is created when the function or special form is entered.

A direct solution to the functional argument problem that also prevents any global-local name conflicts is to program the built-in LAMBDA and SPECIAL forms to scan through the argument list and body of each function and special form being defined and substitute a unique new name for each formal argument name at each occurrence. These unique names could be formed from an increasing counter and a nonprinting character joined with the user-specified name. Of course, the original user-specified name should be kept for printing-out purposes. The effect of this would be to change the LISP temporal binding rule so that each ordinary atom is bound as early as possible, while still maintaining a call-time binding regime. This earliest binding time cannot be at the time of definition, but it can be just before a function or special form is applied to arguments at the top level of the LISP interpreter.

> **Exercise 19.2:** How does this device of using unique formal argument names compare with using the Algol substitution rule for function calls instead of the LISP association list binding rule?

In practice the functional argument problem is not serious. Discipline and due care in choosing names is all that is needed to avoid trouble. Of course in a language like C, there is no chance of trouble to begin with.

> **Exercise 19.3:** Explain how the function M defined here works:
> (SETQ M (LAMBDA (M X) (M X))). Describe the contexts in
> which this function fails to work.

Some versions of LISP use a rule for evaluating selected atoms that relegates the association list to a lower priority. Such a high-priority atom is evaluated by looking at its global atom table value first, and then, only if this is undefined, is the association list searched. This exception is annoyingly nonuniform, so we use strictly temporal binding here. Note, however, that this approach of relegating association list bindings to be of lower priority than global atom table bindings for selected atoms ensures that atoms like NIL and PLUS can be forced to always have their familiar values (except if explicit SETQ operations are done, and even this can be restricted). A similar variation is commonly found where an atom's global atom table value is used whenever that value is a function or special form and the atom is being used as such. Another kind of binding rule, instead of call-time binding, is often used in LISP, where the free variables in a function body are bound, with respect to that function body only, at the time the function is computed. This requires that a tree of association lists or other equivalent structures be maintained. Indeed the elaborate binding rules that have been introduced into current LISP dialects to "cure" perceived anomalies constitute one of the major areas of extension of LISP.

Exercise 19.4: Explain how the following function B, defined below, works on number arguments.

```
(SETQ B (LAMBDA (NIL)
                (COND ((GREATERP NIL 0) T)
                (T 'NIL)))).
```

Solution 19.4: It works just fine.

Searching for a formal argument atom in a linear association list can be time-consuming. Another strategy for binding values to formal argument atoms, which is called *shallow binding*, is a preferable way to handle argument binding. With shallow binding, whenever a value is to be bound to an ordinary atom, we arrange to save the present value of the ordinary atom at the top of a corresponding private push-down list associated with that atom. After having introduced such private push-down lists, argument binding may then be done by first pushing the current value of each ordinary atom to be bound, together with its typecode, on its corresponding push-down list, and then reassigning the values of each such atom in order to effect the bindings. When a user-defined function or special form has been evaluated, the unbinding that restores the previous context is done by popping the push-down list of each formal argument ordinary atom. Shallow call-time binding is used in the LISP interpreter program, given below.

The operation of binding a value, represented by a typed-pointer p, as the current value of an ordinary atom is similar to the effect of the SETQ function, but not identical. In particular, if p is a type 14 or 15 typed-pointer, it is *not* transmuted into a type 12 or 13 type-pointer. Moreover, a doubly indirect type 12 or 13 typed-pointer *is* transmuted by one level of dereferencing into the index of the list area node where the associated (argument list, body) dotted-pair resides, and this index, together with the associated typecode 12 or 13, becomes the current value of the ordinary atom being bound. These binding transmutation rules are appropriate because binding a function value to a formal argument atom is the act of associating a set of ordered pairs with the formal argument atom.

The name, if any, of a function is not preserved by binding, however. Thus, the act of binding a named function to a formal argument atom causes that function to temporarily have a new name. For example, typing in ((LAMBDA (X) X) PLUS) results in {builtin function: X} being printing out.

> **Exercise 19.5:** How does a recursive function, like FACT, continue to work when it is bound to another symbol, say G, and then invoked as (G 3)?

Note that the following identities are a consequence of the simple association-list binding rule discussed above:

$$v[((\text{SPECIAL } (X) \ (\text{EVAL } X)) \ Y)] = v[Y], \text{ and}$$
$$v[((\text{LAMBDA } (X) \ X) \ Y)] = v[Y], \text{ but}$$
$$v[((\text{SPECIAL } (X) \ (\text{EVAL } X)) \ X)] = X, \text{ and}$$
$$v[((\text{LAMBDA } (X) \ X) \ X)] = v[X].$$

The identity $v[((\text{SPECIAL } (X) \ (\text{EVAL } X)) \ X)] = X$ demonstrates the distinction between the LISP context-dependent association-list binding rule and the Algol substitution rule in assigning a meaning to a special form. There is no association list with the substitution rule. Substitution of X for X would produce EVAL applied to X, the value of which would then be $v[X]$ as found in the ordinary atom table. The LISP context-dependent binding rule leads us to compute EVAL applied to X, *after* X is bound to X, so that the resulting value is again X. It is not the case that one of these rules is "better" than the other; however, our expectations may be violated when we replace one rule with the other.

> **Exercise 19.6:** What is $v[((\text{LAMBDA } (X) \ (\text{CONS } (\text{SETQ } X \ 2) \ X)) \ 3)]$?
>
> **Solution 19.6:** (2 . 2). When SETQ is used to assign a value to an ordinary atom that is a currently active formal argument, the actual argument value it was bound to is lost. This is, in essence, a dynamic rebinding operation. In the form of LISP corresponding to the LISP interpreter given in this book, it is not possible to change the global atom table value of an atom that is active as a formal argument without introducing a new built-in function for this purpose. We can, however, as just seen, change the value of a *current* bound atom; that new binding will disappear when the function that established the binding is exited.
>
> **Exercise 19.7:** Define a LISP special form FREEVAR, which takes a λ-expression L as input and returns a list of all the atoms in L that are free variables within L.

Exercise 19.8: Explain the difficulty hidden in the following LISP input.

```
(SETQ F1 (LAMBDA (G L) (F2 (CAR L) (CDR L))))
(SETQ F2 (LAMBDA (H L) (CONS (G H) L)))
(SETQ H (LAMBDA (A B) (COND ((NULL A) B)
                            (T (H (CDR A) (PLUS B 1))))))
(F1 H (QUOTE ((1))))
```

Most LISP dialects provide an additional class of functions called *macros*. We could introduce macro-functions by defining a built-in special form called MACRO, which behaves like LAMBDA and SPECIAL, and builds an argument, body dotted-pair in the same manner. Macro functions obey the following evaluation rule. If m is a macro function that has k arguments, then:

$$v[(m\ a_1\ a_2 \dots a_k)] = v[((\text{EVAL (LIST 'SPECIAL (CAR (BODY } m))$$
$$(\text{LIST 'EVAL (CDR (BODY } m)))))\ a_1\ a_2 \dots a_k)].$$

Exercise 19.9: Define a LISP function called MAC, which takes as input a user-defined LISP function f and an argument list w and returns the value of f on the arguments w computed as though f were a macro.

CHAPTER 20

■ ■ ■

Minimal LISP

Let the set of basic S-expressions be the set of ordinary atoms (with nonnumeric names) and non-atomic S-expressions formed from these. The following nine functions and special forms constitute a set of functions and special forms that are universal in the sense that, with these, any computable function of basic S-expression arguments can be expressed:

QUOTE, ATOM, EQ, CONS, CAR, CDR, COND, LAMBDA, LABEL.

Remember that LABEL is really a notational device to allow the statement of recursive λ-expressions, so we might (weakly) say that there are just eight functional components of minimal LISP.

Why would we consider what constitutes a minimal collection of LISP operators? We would never want to use such a silly restricted programming language. The answer is that LISP is not just an unusual, but practical, programming language; it is heavily influenced by the ethos of the *mathematical theory of computation*, where we ask what functions can be computed and how many steps are needed to compute a function in terms of its input. Generally we restrict ourselves to integer domain and range sets. In order to define what a step is, we find it useful to consider simple models of computation such as Turing machines. Minimal LISP is another such computational model.

The computable functions of basic S-expression arguments correspond to the computable functions of nonnegative integers since we can prescribe an effective enumerating mapping that assigns a nonnegative integer to every basic S-expression. It is somewhat easier to show just that the computable functions of nonnegative integers are subsumed by the computable functions of basic S-expression arguments. To do this, we associate the integer k with the atom NIL if k is 0, and with the list (T ... T) consisting of k T's if $k > 0$. Thus nonnegative integers, and by further extension, rational numbers, are, in effect, included in the domains of various minimal LISP functions.

> **Exercise 20.1:** Write the minimal LISP function that corresponds to addition using the number-to-list correspondence stated above. Then do the same for subtraction of a lesser number list from a greater number list.

© Gary D. Knott 2017
G. D. Knott, *Interpreting LISP*, DOI 10.1007/978-1-4842-2707-7_20

Exercise 20.2: Discuss the pros and cons of extending the definitions of CAR and CDR so that $v[(\text{CAR NIL})] = v[(\text{CDR NIL})] = \text{NIL}$.

Exercise 20.3: Do EVAL, ATOM, EQ, CONS, CAR, CDR, COND, SPECIAL, and LABEL constitute a universal LISP minimal system?

CHAPTER 21

More Functions

This chapter discusses more functions and special forms.

- SUM: **function with a varying number of arguments**

  $v[(\text{SUM } n_1 \, n_2 \dots n_k)] = v[(\text{PLUS } n_1 \, (\text{PLUS } n_2 \, (\dots (\text{PLUS } n_k \, 0)) \dots))].$

- PRODUCT: **function with a varying number of arguments**

  $v[(\text{PRODUCT } n_1 \, n_2 \dots n_k)] = v[(\text{TIMES } n_1 \, (\text{TIMES } n_2 \, (\dots (\text{TIMES } n_k \, 1)) \dots))].$

- DO: **function with a varying number of arguments**

  $v[(\text{DO } x_1 \, x_2 \dots x_k)] = v[x_k].$

  Since DO is a function, its arguments are all evaluated from left to right, and the last argument value is then returned. This function is useful when its arguments have side-effects that occur during their evaluation. Basically, DO provides a means to execute a sequence of statements (function applications) as in a traditional programming language.

- INTO: **function**

  Defined by:

  ```
  (SETQ INTO (LAMBDA (G L)
                     (COND ((NULL L) L)
                           (T (CONS (G (CAR L))
                                    (INTO G (CDR L)))))))).
  ```

  Given the list L = $(L_1 \, L_2 \dots L_k)$, the INTO function computes the application of the function or special form G to each element of L to obtain $((\text{G } L_1) \, (\text{G } L_2) \dots (\text{G } L_k))$.

© Gary D. Knott 2017
G. D. Knott, *Interpreting LISP*, DOI 10.1007/978-1-4842-2707-7_21

- ONTO: **function**

  Defined by:

  ```
  (SETQ ONTO (LAMBDA (G L)
                     (COND ((NULL L) L)
                           (T (CONS (G L)
                                    (ONTO G (CDR L))))))).
  ```

  Given the list L = (L_1 L_2 ... L_k), the ONTO function computes the application of the function or special form G to the list L and, recursively, to every tail of L to obtain ((G L) (G (CDR L)) ... (G (CDR (CDR ... (CDR L))))).

- APPLY: **special form**

  Defined by:

  ```
  (SETQ APPLY (SPECIAL (G X) (EVAL (CONS G X)))).
  ```

  Exercise 21.1: Note v[(APPLY CAR ('(1 . 2)))] = 1 and v[(APPLY CONS ('A 'B))] = (A . B). What is v[(APPLY CAR (1 . 2))]? What is v[(APPLY CAR ((1 . 2)))]? What is v[(APPLY CAR '(1 . 2))]? What is v[(DO (SETQ A '(1 . 2)) (APPLY CAR (A)))]? Did you find a bug in the LISP interpreter?

  Exercise 21.2: v[(APPLY G (x_1 ... x_n))] is intended to be the same as v[(G x_1 ... x_n)]. But we may sometimes forget to enclose the arguments x_1, ..., x_n in parentheses. What is wrong with defining APPLY with (SETQ APPLY (SPECIAL (G X) (EVAL (CONS G (LIST X)))))? Can you think of a better solution?

  Exercise 21.3: Can you think of a reason why the name G should be replaced by an unlikely name like $G in the definition of APPLY? Hint: consider the situation where the value of the ordinary atom G is a user-defined function and G is used in a call to APPLY. Why isn't this a problem in INTO and ONTO? Shouldn't X be replaced by an unlikely name also?

  Exercise 21.4: The version of INTO given above only works for functions of one argument. Give a modified version that works for functions of k arguments with a list of k-tuples provided as the other input. Hint: use APPLY.

Exercise 21.5: What is v[MINUS]? What is v[(LIST MINUS 2)]?
What is v[(DO (SETQ H (LAMBDA (H) ((CAR H) (CAR (CDR H))
))) (H (LIST MINUS 2)))]?

Exercise 21.6: Define a LISP function COPYL that takes a single
list L as input and returns a copy of L that shares no nodes
with the input list L.

Exercise 21.7: Define a LISP function NAINX that takes an
atom a and a list x as input and returns the number of times
the atom a occurs at any level in the list x.

Exercise 21.8: Define a LISP function NAINS that takes an
atom a and a non-atomic S-expression x as input and returns
the number of times the atom a occurs in x at any level.

Exercise 21.9: Define a LISP function NEINS1 that takes an
S-expression e and a list s as input and returns the number of
times e occurs as an element of the list s.

Exercise 21.10: Define a LISP function NEINSX that takes an
S-expression e and a list s as input and returns the number of
times e occurs as an element of the list s or as an element of
any list occurring in the list s at any level, including s itself.

Exercise 21.11: Define the LISP function UNION that takes two
lists x and y as input and returns the list z whose elements are
the elements of the set union of x and y (i.e., the result is to
contain only unique elements).

Exercise 21.12: Define the LISP function SORT that takes a list
of numbers as input and returns the corresponding sorted list
of numbers as the result.

Solution 21.12:

```
(SETQ SORT
(LAMBDA (X)
        (COND ((NULL X) X)
                (T (LABEL MERGE
                        (LAMBDA (V L)
                                (COND ((OR (NULL L) (LESSP V (CAR L)))
                                        (CONS V L))
                                        (T (CONS (CAR L)
                                                (MERGE V (CDR L)))))))
                (CAR X) (SORT (CDR X))))))) )
```

Note LABEL is used here, so you will have to define MERGE as a separate function if you want to try this in the LISP interpreter as given below.

Exercise 21.13: Define the LISP function SIGMA that takes a number-valued function g of an integer argument as input, together with two integers a and b as additional input, and which returns the value $\displaystyle\sum_{a\le i\le b} g(i)$

Solution 21.13:

```
(SETQ SIGMA (LAMBDA (G A B)
                    (COND ((LESSP B A) 0)
                          (T (PLUS (G A) (SIGMA G (PLUS A 1) B))))))))
```

SIGMA computes $\displaystyle\sum_{A\le I\le B} G(i)$ where G is a real-valued function of a single argument.

Exercise 21.14: Define the LISP function FACTORS that takes an integer n as input and returns a list consisting of the prime factors of n.

Let's consider constructing a WHILE statement in LISP. A WHILE statement should repetitively evaluate some S-expression q until some other S-expression p evaluates to NIL. For example, assuming we define WHILE as a special form with two arguments P and Q, we should be able to execute:

```
(SETQ I 0)
(SETQ S 2)
(WHILE (LESSP I S) (DO (SETQ I (PLUS I 1)) (PRINT (LIST I))))
```

and observe (1) (2) printed out.

Note that for WHILE to terminate nontrivially, it will be necessary for the evaluation of the actual arguments corresponding to P and/or Q to involve some side-effect that leads to the value of the actual argument corresponding to P becoming NIL at some point. Such a side-effect can be obtained by using SETQ, PUTPROP, REMPROP, RPLACA, or RPLACD.

Here is one way to define WHILE.

- WHILE: **special form**

   Defined by:

```
(SETQ WHILE (SPECIAL (P Q)
                     (COND ((EVAL P)
                            (DO (EVAL Q) (EVAL (LIST 'WHILE P Q) ))))))
```

$v[(\text{WHILE } p\ q)] = \text{NIL}$, if $(\text{WHILE } p\ q)$ terminates. If $v[p]$ is initially NIL, NIL is returned. Otherwise the argument q is evaluated repeatedly until $v[p]$ becomes NIL. Generally a side-effect that induces a change in the value of p is required for WHILE to terminate.

Exercise 21.15: What is wrong with defining WHILE via:

```
(SETQ WHILE (SPECIAL (P Q)
                (COND ((EVAL P)
                        (DO (EVAL Q) (WHILE (EVAL P) (EVAL Q)) )))))?
```

Exercise 21.16: We may define WHILE via:

```
(SETQ WHILE (SPECIAL (P Q)
                (COND ((EVAL P)
                        (DO (EVAL Q) (EVAL (CDR (BODY WHILE)))) ))))
```

Explain why this works. Hint: review skip-binding.

CHAPTER 22

Input and Output

In order to be able to specify a LISP function that behaves like an interactive program, we need a mechanism for printing messages to a user and for reading user-supplied input. The functions READ and PRINT satisfy these requirements.

- READ: **pseudo-function**

  $v[(READ)]$ equals the S-expression, which is typed in response to the prompt exclamation mark symbol ! typed to the user.

- PRINT: **function with a varying number of arguments and innocuous side-effects**

  $v[(PRINT\ x_1\ x_2 \dots x_k)] = NIL$, with $v[x_1]$, $v[x_2]$, ... , $v[x_k]$ each printed out at the terminal as a side-effect. If k is 0, a single blank is printed out.

- PRINTCR: **function with a varying number of arguments and innocuous side-effects**

  $v[(PRINTCR\ x_1\ x_2 \dots x_k)] = NIL$, with $v[x_1]$, $v[x_2]$, ... , $v[x_k]$ each followed by a carriage-return and printed out at the terminal as a side-effect. If k is 0, a single carriage-return is printed out. (A *carriage-return* is an old-fashioned way of saying newline. On Linux or OS-X, a newline is an ASCII linefeed(10); on Windows, a newline is actually the two ASCII characters carriage-return(13) followed by a linefeed(10)).

© Gary D. Knott 2017
G. D. Knott, *Interpreting LISP*, DOI 10.1007/978-1-4842-2707-7_22

CHAPTER 23

■ ■ ■

Property Lists

Ordinary atoms have values, and it is often convenient to imagine that an ordinary atom has several values. This can be accomplished by making a list of these values and using this list as *the* value whose elements are the desired several values. Frequently, however, these multiple values are used to encode *properties*. This is so common that LISP provides special features to accommodate properties.

Abstractly, a property is a function. LISP only provides for properties that apply to ordinary atoms and whose values are S-expressions, and it establishes and uses a special set of lists to tabulate input-output pairs of such properties. Suppose A is an ordinary atom and *g* is an abstract property function. Then the value of *g* on A is called the *g-property value* of A. Rather than computing a particular property value of an atom when it is needed, LISP provides a means to record such property values along with the corresponding ordinary atom, so that a property value may be retrieved rather than computed.

Each ordinary atom A has an associated list provided called the *property list* of A. The typed-pointer to this list is stored in the plist field of the ordinary atom A. This list may be thought of as an *alternate value* of A. Generally the property list of an ordinary atom A is either NIL, or it is a list of dotted-pairs. Each such dotted-pair, $(p \cdot w)$, in the property list for A is interpreted as meaning that the value of property *p* on A is *w*. Thus properties and property values are represented by S-expressions. In fact, usually properties are represented by ordinary atoms.

The following functions are provided in order to aid in handling property lists.

- PUTPROP: **function with a side-effect**

    $v[(\text{PUTPROP } a\ p\ w)] = v[a]$, and the property, property-value dotted-pair $(v[p] \cdot v[w])$ is inserted in the property list for the atom $v[a]$. If another duplicate property, property-value dotted-pair for the property $v[p]$ and the property-value $v[w]$, is present, it is removed. $v[a]$ must be an ordinary atom, and $v[p]$ and $v[w]$ are arbitrary S-expressions.

© Gary D. Knott 2017
G. D. Knott, *Interpreting LISP*, DOI 10.1007/978-1-4842-2707-7_23

- GETPROP: **function**

  $v[(\text{GETPROP } a\ p)]$ equals the current property value, which is dotted with the property $v[p]$ on the property list for the ordinary atom $v[a]$. If a dotted-pair for the property $v[p]$ does not exist on the property list of $v[a]$, then NIL is returned.

- REMPROP: **function with a side-effect**

  $v[(\text{REMPROP } a\ p\ w)] = v[a]$, and the property, property-value dotted-pair $(v[p] . v[w])$ for the property $v[p]$ is removed from the property list of the ordinary atom $v[a]$ if such a dotted-pair exists on the property list for $v[a]$.

  Exercise 23.1: Define a special form called SPUTPROP analogous to PUTPROP, which does not have its arguments evaluated.

  Solution 23.1: (SETQ SPUTPROP (SPECIAL (A P W) (PUTPROP A P W))).

The functions PUTPROP, GETPROP, and REMPROP can all be defined in terms of the basic built-in functions GETPLIST and PUTPLIST, where $v[(\text{GETPLIST } a)]$ equals the property list for the ordinary atom $v[a]$, and where $v[(\text{PUTPLIST } a\ s)] = v[a]$, with the side-effect that the property list of the ordinary atom $v[a]$ is replaced with the list $v[s]$. Now PUTPROP, GETPROP, and REMPROP are definable as follows:

```
(SETQ GETPROP (LAMBDA (A P)
                    (ASSOC (GETPLIST A) P)))

(SETQ ASSOC (LAMBDA (L P)
                  (COND ((NULL L) NIL)
                        (T (COND ((EQUAL P (CAR (CAR L))) (CDR (CAR L)))
                                 (T (ASSOC (CDR L) P)))))))

(SETQ REMPROP (LAMBDA (A P W)
                    (PUTPLIST A (NPROP NIL (GETPLIST A) (CONS P W)))))

(SETQ NPROP (LAMBDA (H L P)
                  (COND ((NULL L) (REVERSE H))
                        ((EQUAL P (CAR L)) (APPEND (REVERSE H) (CDR L)))
                        (T (NPROP (CONS (CAR L) H) (CDR L) P)))))

(SETQ PUTPROP (LAMBDA (A P W)
                    (PUTPLIST A (CONS (CONS P W)
                                      (GETPLIST (REMPROP A P W))))))
```

Exercise 23.2: Why don't we define PUTPROP as:

```
(LAMBDA (A P W)
        (COND ((EQ (GETPROP A P) W) A)
              (T (PUTLIST (CONS (CONS P W)
                                (GETPLIST A))))))?
```

Exercise 23.3: Can the same property-value pair occur on the same property list several times?

Solution 23.3: No, not if only PUTPROP is used to build property lists. And, in fact, REMPROP assumes duplicates are not present.

Exercise 23.4: Why is REVERSE used in NPROP? Is it necessary?

Exercise 23.5: Give definitions of PUTPROP, GETPROP, and REMPROP, so that properties can be relations rather than just functions. Thus multiple $(p \cdot w)$ dotted-pairs occurring on the same property list with the same p-value and differing w-values are to be handled properly.

Solution 23.5: Only GETPROP needs redefinition, so that it returns a list of property values. It may be a beneficial practice to keep all properties functional, however. This is no real hardship, since, for example, (COLORS . RED), (COLORS . BLUE), and (COLORS . GREEN) can be recast as (COLORS . (RED BLUE GREEN)).

Exercise 23.6: One useful device that is commonly used is to specify class subset relations with T-valued properties. For example, we might execute:

```
(PUTPROP 'MEN 'MORTAL T),
(PUTPROP 'MAN 'MEN T), and
(PUTPROP 'SOCRATES 'MAN T).
```

But note that $v[$(GETPROP 'SOCRATES 'MORTAL)$]$ equals NIL. (Also note that $v[$(GETPROP 'MEN 'MORTAL)$] = $ T and $v[$(GETPROP MEN MORTAL)$]$ are undefined.

Write a LISP function LINKGETPROP, which will trace all property lists of atom properties with the associated value T reachable from the property list of an input atom A in order to find the specified property value pair (P,T) and return T when this pair is found. The value NIL is to be returned when no chain leads to the sought-for property P with a T value. Thus, for example, with the properties for MEN, MAN, and SOCRATES given above, (LINKGETPROP 'SOCRATES 'MORTAL) returns T; essentially (LINKGETPROP 'A 'P) asks if there is a chain of property "assertions" that implies *A* has the property P *indirectly*.

Solution 23.6:

```
(SETQ LINKGETPROP (LAMBDA (A P)
                      (COND ((EQ (GETPROP A P) T) T)
                            (T (SEARCH (GETPLIST A) P)))))

(SETQ SEARCH (LAMBDA (L P)
                 (COND ((NULL L) L)
                       ((AND (EQ (CDR (CAR L)) T)
                             (ATOM (CAR (CAR L)))
                             (EQ (LINKGETPROP (CAR (CAR L)) P) T)) T)
                       (T (SEARCH (CDR L) P)))))
```

Exercise 23.7: Write a LISP function CKPROP such that (CKPROP *a p w*) returns T if ($v[p]$. $v[w]$) is on the property list for the atom $v[a]$ and NIL otherwise. Now write a generalized form of CKPROP called TCPROP, which is defined such that (TCPROP *a p w*) returns T if there exists a sequence of atoms $m_0, m_1, ... ,$ m_k, with $k \geq 1$, such that $v[a] = m_0$, $v[w] = m_k$, and ($v[p]$. m_{i+1}) is on the property list of m_i for $i = 0, 1, ... , k - 1$. TC stands for *transitive closure*.

The property-list functions defined above, especially REMPROP, and hence PUTPROP, are slow, and moreover they can create lots of garbage unreachable list-nodes. It would be more efficient if we could just *change* property lists as required, rather than rebuild them with CONSing each time a REMPROP is done.

There are two low-level functions with side-effects defined in LISP that provide the ability to *change* existing list-nodes that have been created with CONS. These functions are RPLACA and RPLACD.

- RPLACA: **function with a side-effect**

  $v[(\text{RPLACA } x\, y)] = v[x]$, *after* the *car* field of the list node representing the dotted-pair $v[x]$ is *changed* to the typed-pointer $v[y]$.

- RPLACD: **function with a side-effect**

  $v[(\text{RPLACD } x\,y)] = v[x]$, *after* the *cdr* field of the list node representing the dotted-pair $v[x]$ is *changed* to the typed-pointer $v[y]$.

  Now REMPROP can be programmed as follows:

  ```
  (SETQ REMPROP (LAMBDA (A P W)
                         (PUTPLIST A (NAX (GETPLIST A) (CONS P W)))))

  (SETQ NAX (LAMBDA (L P)
                     (COND ((NULL L) NIL)
                           ((EQUAL (CAR L) P) (CDR L))
                           (T (DO (NX L P) L)))))

  (SETQ NX (LAMBDA (L P)
                    (COND ((NULL (CDR L)) NIL)
                          ((EQUAL P (CAR (CDR L))) (RPLACD L (CDR L)))
                          (T (NX (CDR L) P)))))
  ```

  Exercise 23.8: Could NX be defined with an empty formal argument list ( ) rather than (L P), and be called as (NX) in NAX?

Note this version of REMPROP can only be safely used when we can guarantee that the backbone nodes of property lists are not shared within other list structures.

  Exercise 23.9: Program a version of APPEND, called NCONC, which uses RPLACD to append one list onto another by physical relinking.

CHAPTER 24

■ ■ ■

What Is LISP Good for?

The quick answer to the question "What is LISP good for?" is (1) ideas and (2) experimental programs.

The algorithmic ideas that LISP inspires are often powerful and elegant. Even if LISP is not the target programming language, thinking about how to tackle a programming job using LISP can pay worthwhile dividends in ideas for data structures, for the use of recursion, and for functional programming approaches. The use of Algol-like languages or FORTRAN tends to limit programmers' imagination, and both applications programmers and systems programmers can benefit by remembering the principles of LISP.

LISP is useful for building and trying out programs to solve predominantly nonnumeric problems such as natural language parsing or dialog processing, symbolic formula manipulation, retrieval in a LISP-encoded database, theorem proving, backtrack searching (e.g., game playing), and pattern recognition programs.

Most versions of LISP have been extended with arrays, strings, a FORTRAN-like statement-based programming facility via the so-called PROG special form, and many other features. Indeed, the enthusiasm for extending LISP is perennially high. Many extensions take the form of control structures and data structures for managing abstract search. As LISP is extended, however, it seems to lose its sparse pure elegance and uniform view of data. The added features are sometimes baroquely complex, and the programmers' mental burden is correspondingly increased. Moreover, at some point it is legitimate to ask why not extend FORTRAN or C to contain LISP features, rather than conversely? And indeed this has also been done.

Often features are added to LISP to increase its speed. The standard accessing strategy in LISP is, in essence, linear searching through non-atomic S-expressions, and many attempts have been made to circumvent this. LISP with extensions, then, is likely to be a curious amalgam of considerable complexity, sometimes with the possibility of constructing faster programs as a compensating factor. (Although, if a program is perceived to be fast enough by its users, then it is fast enough, no matter what language it is written in.)

Not only does LISP perform slowly in comparison to conventional loop-based programs, but it is also designed as a self-contained programming system. Thus, like APL, it may be difficult to employ and/or control computer system resources, access files, and handle interrupts in a general and convenient manner. In short, without suitable extensions, LISP is not a systems programming tool, and insofar as a program must deal with such environmental issues, LISP is generally inadequate to the challenge. Since most programs with a long half-life have systems programming aspects, LISP is generally not the tool of

© Gary D. Knott 2017
G. D. Knott, *Interpreting LISP*, DOI 10.1007/978-1-4842-2707-7_24

choice for building a robust, efficient system for long-term use. Note, however, system programming extensions can be added to LISP by introducing suitable "hooks" to the operating system; the well-known *emacs* text editor is written in an extended version of LISP.

Minor details also mitigate against LISP. Format control for terminal input and output is often lacking, for example, and this can be frustrating in many applications. Moreover, although LISP list notation is adequate for short functions (indeed, it encourages them), it is cumbersome compared to Algol notation, and the lack of traditional mathematical notation is a severe handicap in many cases. Notational extensions have been proposed, but again, simplicity is sacrificed.

On the other hand, LISP is an excellent tool for experimentation. A pattern-matching idea may be programmed and tested in a preliminary way more easily and quickly in LISP than in Pascal, for example. The lack of a variety of constrained datatypes and the absence of declarations and multiple statement forms often give an advantage to LISP as long as we banish efficiency considerations from our minds. Moreover, there are certain applications, notably formula manipulation tasks, where S-expressions and recursion are so well suited for the job that LISP matches the utility of any other language.

Unfortunately, many versions of LISP do not gracefully cohabit with programs written in other programming languages, so a system can't generally be easily constructed that employs LISP just for selected subtasks. However, a special embeddable LISP interpreter could be relatively easily constructed as a C or FORTRAN callable subroutine package, which would allow the use of LISP for specialized purposes within a larger non-LISP system. (Indeed, you could modify the LISP interpreter program to read its input from a memory array rather than a file or the keyboard, and thereby achieve such a LISP subroutine.)

We shall consider several classical applications of LISP in the chapters that follow.

CHAPTER 25

■ ■ ■

Symbolic Differentiation

The rules for differentiation are explicitly recursive, so it is easy to use LISP to compute the symbolic derivative of a real-valued function of real-number arguments. The biggest difficulty is the problem of input and output notation. If we agree to accept the LISP prefix notation for algebraic expressions, so that we enter $1 + sin(x + y)/x$ as (PLUS 1 (QUOTIENT (APPLY SIN ((PLUS $x\,y$))) x)) for example, then the task of differentiation is truly simple. But if we instead demand that the input and output be in traditional infix form, the job becomes more complicated.

We shall present a collection of LISP functions and special forms that provide the ability to define, differentiate, and print out elementary real-valued functions of real arguments. These LISP functions and special forms include FSET, DIFF, and FPRINT.

We will use the special form FSET to define a real-valued function of real arguments by typing (FSET G (X Y...) (f)), where G is an ordinary atom, (X Y...) is a list of ordinary atoms denoting the formal arguments of the function G being defined, and f is an *infix* form, which is the body that defines G. For example, (FSET G1 (X Y) (X + Y * EXP(X))) defines the function G1(X , Y) = X + Y * EXP(X) in proper LISP prefix form as established by using SETQ with the appropriate λ-expression. The idea of FSET is to construct and execute the LISP S-expression, which defines the function expressed in the input to FSET; for example, (FSET G1 (X Y) (X + Y * EXP(X))) constructs (SETQ G1 (LAMBDA (X Y) (PLUS X (TIMES Y (APPLY EXP (X)))))), which is then executed (i.e., evaluated).

Note that an infix form here is a kind of pun; it denotes the intended algebraic expression and it also is a particular LISP S-expression. The only caveat is that blanks must delimit operators in infix forms to ensure that they will be interpreted as atoms within the S-expression. We use the FORTRAN notation * for multiplication and ** for exponentiation.

Such a function can be differentiated with respect to a variable, which may be either a free variable or a formal argument. The derivative is itself a function that has the same formal arguments. The derivative of such an FSET-defined function G with respect to X is denoted G#X. The LISP function DIFF will be defined to compute the derivative of such a real-valued function, G, with respect to a specified symbol X, and store the resulting function as the value of the created atom G#X. This is done for a function G by typing (DIFF G X).

In order to construct atoms with names like G#X, which depend upon the names of other atoms, we will use the built-in LISP function MKATOM, which makes atoms whose names are composed from the names of other atoms. MKATOM is defined such that $v[($MKATOM$\,x\,y)]$ equals the ordinary atom whose name is the string formed by concatenating the names of the ordinary atoms $v[x]$ and $v[y]$.

© Gary D. Knott 2017
G. D. Knott, *Interpreting LISP*, DOI 10.1007/978-1-4842-2707-7_25

Functions defined by FSET or by DIFF may be printed out for examination by using the LISP function FPRINT, as defined below.

A function H defined by FSET or DIFF may be evaluated at the point $(x_1, x_2, \dots)$, where $x_1, x_2, \dots$ are numbers, by using APPLY. Thus, typing (APPLY H $(x_1 x_2 \dots)$) causes the number $H(x_1, x_2, \dots)$ to be printed out. Of course, all the subsidiary functions called in H must be defined as well.

The differentiation rules used by DIFF are as follows. The symbol D denotes differentiation with respect to a specific understood ordinary atom variable name x, called the symbol of D, as shown in the following:

```
D(A + B)   = D(A) + D(B)
D(A - B)   = D(A) - D(B)
D(-A)      = -D(A)
D(A * B)   = A * D(B) + B * D(A)
D(A/B)     = D(A)/B + A * D(B * *(-1))
D(A * *B) = B * A * *(B - 1) * D(A) + LOG(A) * A * *B * D(B)   (** denotes exponentiation)
D(LOG(A)) = D(A)/A
```

If F(X Y ...) has been defined via FSET, then we use the chain rule:

```
D(F(A B ... )) = F#X(A B ... ) * D(A) + F#Y(A B ... ) * D(B) + ....
```

If A is an ordinary atom variable then D(A) = 1 if A is the symbol of D, and D(A) = 0 otherwise.

If A is a number, then D(A) = 0.

The infix forms used to define functions with FSET are translated into corresponding S-expressions, which will be called E-expressions in order to distinguish them in discourse. E-expressions are made up of evaluatable prefix S-expressions involving numbers and ordinary atoms and other E-expressions.

The basic LISP functional forms used in E-expressions are:

(MINUS a)

(PLUS a b)

(DIFFERENCE a b)

(TIMES a b)

(QUOTIENT a b), (POWER a b), where a and b are E-expressions

(APPLY h $(x_1 x_2 \dots)$), where $x_1, x_2, \dots$ are E-expressions, and h is an FSET-defined or DIFF-defined function.

The definitions of FSET, DIFF, and FPRINT follow.

- FSET: **special form**

  $v[(\text{FSET G (X Y ...) } (e))] = v[\text{G}]$ where G is an ordinary atom whose name does not begin with \$, and (X Y ...) is a list of atoms that are the formal arguments to the function G being defined. e is an infix functional form that is used to define G(X, Y, ...). As mentioned above, (FSET G (X Y ...) (e)) defines G to be a function of the arguments X Y ... whose *body* is given by the *infix* expression (e). The list (e) will be parsed and converted into a proper λ-expression used to define the value of the atom G.

FSET is defined by:

```
(SETQ FSET (SPECIAL ($G $L $Q)
                    (SET $G (EVAL (LIST 'LAMBDA $L (ELIST $Q))))))
```

The function SET has been defined above. Here we redefine SET by:

```
(SETQ SET (LAMBDA ($X $Y)
                  (EVAL (CONS 'SETQ (CONS $X (CONS '$Y NIL)))))))
```

Exercise 25.1: Why are such strange formal argument names used to define FSET and SET? Hint: think about using SETQ to assign values to ordinary atoms, which are active formal arguments. In particular, suppose the \$-signs were dropped, and we executed (FSET Y (X) X)?

Exercise 25.2: Can you think of a way to allow the user to write (FSET Y (X) = e)? Note the third argument here is =.

ELIST constructs the E-expression corresponding to its argument by using the Bauer-Samelson-Ershov postfix Polish translation algorithm [SB60, Ers59]. ELIST is also used to process the argument of a unary minus operation.

Exercise 25.3: Use a library or, if you must, a web search to find out about *Jan Łukasiewicz* and about Polish notation.

```
(SETQ ELIST (LAMBDA (L)
                    (COND ((ATOM L) L)
                          ((EQ (CDR L) NIL) (ELIST (CAR L)))
                          (T (EP NIL NIL (DLIST L)))))))
```

```
(SETQ DLIST (LAMBDA (L)
                 (COND ((ATOM L) L)
                       ((NULL (CDR L)) (DLIST (CAR L)))
                       (T L))))
```

(EP OP P L) is the result of completing the Polish translation of L using the stacks OP and P.

```
(SETQ EP (LAMBDA (OP P L)
              (COND ((NULL L) (COND ((NULL OP) (DLIST P))
                                    (T (BUILD OP P L))))
                    (T (POLISH OP P (CAR L) (CDR L))))))
```

```
(SETQ CADR (LAMBDA (L) (CAR (CDR L))))
```

(BUILD OP P L) puts the phrase ((CAR OP) P_2 P_1) on the P stack in place of P_1 and P_2, and goes back to EP to continue the translation.

```
(SETQ BUILD (LAMBDA (OP P L)
                 (EP (CDR OP) (CONS (LIST (NAME (CAR OP))
                                          (CADR P)
                                          (CAR P))
                                    (CDR (CDR P))) L)))
```

In (POLISH OP P B L), B is the current input symbol, and L is the remaining infix input. Either B is to be pushed on OP or else B is used to make a phrase reduction, and a corresponding entry is placed on the P stack.

```
(SETQ POLISH (LAMBDA (OP P B L)
                  (COND ((EQ B '-)
                         (H (LIST 'MINUS (ELIST (CAR L))) (CDR L)))
                        ((NOT (ATOM B)) (H (ELIST B) L))
                        ((NOT (MEMBER B '(+ : * / **)))
                         (COND ((OR (NULL L) (ATOM (CAR L))) (H B L))
                               (T (H (LIST 'APPLY B (INTO ELIST (CAR L)))
                                     (CDR L)))))
                        ((OR (NULL OP) (CKLESS (CAR OP) B))
                         (POLISH (CONS B OP) P (CAR L) (CDR L)))
                        (T (BUILD OP P (CONS B L))))))
```

(H V L) pushes V onto the P stack and goes back to EP. It also changes a binary minus sign at the front of L to the unambiguous internal code : .

```
(SETQ H (LAMBDA (V L)
             (EP OP (CONS (COND ((AND (NOT (ATOM V))
                                      (NULL (CDR V))) (CAR V))
                                (T V))
                          P)
```

```
                  (COND ((AND (NOT (NULL L))
                              (EQ '- (CAR L))) (CONS ': (CDR L)))
                        (T L)))))
(SETQ CKLESS (LAMBDA (A B)
                (COND ((EQ '** A) NIL)
                      ((OR (EQ '* A) (EQ '/ A))
                       (COND ((EQ '** B) T)
                             (T NIL)))
                      ((OR (EQ '+ B) (EQ ': B)) NIL)
                      (T T))))
(SETQ NAME (LAMBDA (A)
                (ASSO A '((** . POWER) (* . TIMES) (/ . QUOTIENT)
                          (: . DIFFERENCE) (+ . PLUS)))))
(SETQ ASSO (LAMBDA (A L)
                (COND ((NULL L) L)
                      ((EQ A (CAR (CAR L))) (CDR (CAR L)))
                      (T (ASSO A (CDR L))))))
```

- FPRINT: **special form**

  $v[(\text{FPRINT } G)] = \text{NIL}$, and the E-expression value of the function-valued atom G is printed out in infix form.

  FPRINT is defined by:

```
(SETQ FPRINT (SPECIAL ($G)
                (DO (PRINT $G (CAR (BODY (EVAL $G)))
                          '= (HP (CDR (BODY (EVAL $G)))))
                    (PRINTCR))))

(SETQ HP (LAMBDA (G)
                (COND ((ATOM G) G)
                      ((NULL (CDR G)) (HP (CAR G)))
                      ((EQ (CAR G) 'MINUS) (LIST '- (HP (CADR G))))
                      ((EQ (CAR G) 'APPLY) (LIST (CADR G)
                                                 (INTO HP (CADR
                                                           (CDR G)))))
                      (T (LIST (HP (CADR G)) (OPSYMBOL (CAR G))
                               (HP (CADR (CDR G))))))))

(SETQ OPSYMBOL (LAMBDA (X)
                (ASSO X '((POWER . **) (TIMES . *) (QUOTIENT . /)
                          (DIFFERENCE . -) (PLUS . +)))))
```

- DIFF: **special form**

  $v[(\text{DIFF } G \ X)] = v[G\#X]$, after the function G#X is defined as a side-effect, where G is a known function and X is an ordinary atom.

DIFF is defined by:

```
(SETQ DIFF (SPECIAL ($G X)
                    (SET (MKATOM $G (MKATOM '# X))
                         (EVAL (LIST 'LAMBDA (CAR (BODY (EVAL $G)))
                               (DI (CDR (BODY (EVAL $G))) X))))))
```

(DI G X) is the E-expression form derivative of the E-expression G with respect to the atom X.

```
(SETQ DI (LAMBDA (E X)
                 (COND ((ATOM E) (COND ((EQ E X) 1) (T 0)))
                       ((NULL (CDR E)) (DI (CAR E) X))
                       (T (DF (CAR E) (CDR E) X)))))

(SETQ DF (LAMBDA (OP L X)
                 (COND ((EQ OP 'MINUS) (LIST OP (DI (CAR L) X)))
                       ((EQ OP 'PLUS) (LIST OP (DI (CAR L) X)
                                           (DI (CADR L) X)))
                       ((EQ OP 'DIFFERENCE) (LIST OP (DI (CAR L) X)
                                                 (DI (CADR L) X)))
                       ((EQ OP 'TIMES) (LIST 'PLUS
                                             (LIST OP (DI (CAR L) X) (CADR L))
                                             (LIST OP (CAR L)
                                                   (DI (CADR L) X))))
                       ((EQ OP 'QUOTIENT) (LIST 'PLUS
                                                (LIST OP (DI (CAR L) X)
                                                      (CADR L))
                                                (LIST 'TIMES (CAR L)
                                                      (DI (LIST 'POWER
                                                                (CADR L) -1)
                                                          X))))
                       ((EQ OP 'POWER) (LIST 'PLUS
                                             (LIST 'TIMES (CADR L)
                                                   (LIST 'TIMES
                                                         (DI (CAR L) X)
                                                         (LIST 'POWER (CAR L)
                                                               (LIST 'DIFFERENCE
                                                                     (CADR L)
                                                                     1))))
                                             (LIST 'TIMES
                                                   (LIST 'APPLY 'LOG
                                                         (LIST (CAR L)))
                                                   (LIST 'TIMES
                                                         (DI (CADR L) X)
                                                         (LIST 'POWER
                                                               (CAR L)
                                                               (CADR L)))))))
                       ((EQ OP 'APPLY)
                        (COND ((EQ (CAR L) 'LOG)
                               (LIST 'QUOTIENT (DI (CADR L) X) (CADR L)))
```

```
                (T (CHAIN (CAR L) (CAR (BODY (EVAL (CAR L))))
                         (CADR L) (CADR L) X)))))))

(SETQ CHAIN (LAMBDA (F A B R X)
                    (COND ((NULL (CDR A)) (TERM F A B R X))
                          (T (LIST 'PLUS (TERM F A B R X)
                                   (CHAIN F (CDR A) B (CDR B) X))))))

(SETQ TERM (LAMBDA (F A B R X)
                   (LIST 'TIMES (DI (CAR R) X)
                         (LIST 'APPLY (MKATOM F (MKATOM '# (CAR A))) B))))
```

Exercise 25.4: Would it be okay to define TERM as

```
(LAMBDA (A R) (LIST 'TIMES (DI (CAR R) X)
                    (LIST 'APPLY (MKATOM F (MKATOM '# (CAR A))) B))),
```

and appropriately modify the associated calls?

Exercise 25.5: Is it necessary to use APPLY to compute functions at particular points? Is it necessary to use APPLY embedded in the bodies of functions created by FSET and DIFF at all?

Solution 25.5: The functions built by FSET and DIFF are full-fledged LISP functions. The use of APPLY could be dispensed with, except that we then need to provide the function LOG, which is used in DIFF. Also, this would avoid the need to watch for the formal argument names used in the special form APPLY in order to avoid the special form functional binding problem. Using APPLY is convenient, however, since we then do not have to distinguish user function names from operator names such as PLUS and TIMES.

Exercise 25.6: The function DF allows products with 1 and sums and differences with 0 to be created. Write a modified version of DF that uses some auxiliary functions to simplify the E-expressions being formed so as to avoid such needless operations.

Exercise 25.7: Introduce the elementary functions EXP, SIN, and COS and implement the explicit differentiation rules that apply to them.

CHAPTER 26

■ ■ ■

Game Playing

In this chapter we will discuss writing a LISP program to play a *zero-sum, perfect-information* game. A perfect-information game is a game such as chess where the entire state of the game (i.e., the current position and its history) is known to all players. Poker is not a perfect-information game. A zero-sum game is just a game where if the game were played for money, then the sum of the winnings and losses is necessarily zero. Poker is a zero-sum game.

A *fair* game is a game where, for perfect players, the expected return to each player in points or money is 0. No one knows whether or not chess is a fair game. We need not assume that we are playing a fair game.

We shall also assume that:

1. The game we wish to program is played by two players making alternate moves.

2. Each position p is either *terminal*, in which case it represents a win, loss, or tie for each player as defined by the rules of the game; or, *non-terminal*, in which case it has a finite, non-zero number of successor positions, among which the player who is to move from position p must select.

3. Every game must eventually reach a terminal position.

These hypotheses are satisfied by many games, although in chess, the rules are such that the position must be considered to include not only the current locations of the pieces and the specification of which player is to move, but also the past history of the game. This is required in the rules for castling, capturing *en passant*, and draw by repetition.

By tradition, one player is called *box*, and a position from which *box* is to move is denoted by a *box* symbol: □. Such a position is called a □ position. The other player is called *circle*, and a position from which *circle* is to move is denoted by a circle symbol: ○. Such a position is called a ○ position.

Terminal positions will be assigned *values* so that the *value* of a □ or ○ terminal position is 1 if the player *box* has won in that position and –1 if the player *circle* has won in that position. If tie terminal positions exist, we assign them the value 0. This means that *box* plays to *maximize* the value of the final terminal position, and *circle* plays to *minimize*

© Gary D. Knott 2017
G. D. Knott, *Interpreting LISP*, DOI 10.1007/978-1-4842-2707-7_26

the terminal position to be achieved; *box* is called the *maximizing* player, and *circle* is called the *minimizing* player. Thus if we are playing chess and the maximizing player *box* is white, then a terminal position where white is checkmated is a □ position and has the value −1, while a terminal position where black is checkmated is a ○ position and has the value 1. If Nim is being played, where the player who takes the last stone and leaves an empty position consisting of an empty arrangement loses, then the empty position with *box* to move is a □ terminal position, since there are no moves possible, and its value is 1, since *circle* lost by allowing this position to be reached. The empty position with *circle* to move is a ○ terminal position with the value −1.

Because of the assumption that the game is a zero-sum game, we see that we are assigning values to terminal positions entirely from *box's* point of view. Thus if the value of a terminal position is 1, then its value to *box* is 1, and hence by the zero-sum property, its value to *circle* is −1. If, on the other hand, the value of a terminal position is −1, its value to *box* is −1 and hence its value to *circle* is 1. This form of assigning values to positions so that positions with positive values are good for *box* and bad for *circle*, while positions with negative values are good for *circle* and bad for *box*, is known as *asymmetric* valuation.

We would like to assign the values −1, 0, or 1 to all positions that may arise, not just terminal positions; and moreover we would like to assign them consistently in such a way that the value of a position is the value of that position to *box*, so that we continue to use asymmetric valuation. We would achieve this objective as follows.

Let b represent a □ position or a ○ position of the game, and let $n(b)$ be the number of immediate successor positions, which may be achieved by moving from b. Let $a_1, \dots,$ $a_{n(b)}$ be the $n(b)$ successor positions in some particular order. If b is a terminal position, $n(b) = 0$. Finally, when b is a terminal position, let $u(b)$ be the value of b.

Now let's define the value of a position b, not necessarily terminal, as $w(b)$, where $w(b)$ is defined recursively as:

$$w(b) := \begin{cases} u(b) & \text{if } n(b) = 0, \\ \max_{1 \le i \le n(b)} w(a_i) & \text{if } b \text{ is a } \square \text{ position,} \\ \min_{1 \le i \le n(b)} w(a_i) & \text{otherwise.} \end{cases}$$

Hypotheses (1), (2), and (3) listed above ensure that w is well defined.

Note the asymmetry in the definition of w. Note also that the use of w to compute the value of a position b requires that all possible successor positions be valuated first and so on recursively. Thus we must generate the full *game tree* with root b whose leaf nodes are terminal positions that are valued by means of u. Then for each node whose sons all have values, we can back up the minimum or the maximum of these values as may be appropriate to the father node. By iteratively backing up, we may eventually compute the value of b. This process is known as *minimaxing*.

Von Neumann and Morgenstern [NM44] introduced the notion of minimaxing in a game tree in their treatise on game theory. Their purpose was to show that even for multistage games with alternative choices at each stage, any line of play could be considered to be the result of fixed strategies, that is, predetermined plans that could be adopted at the outset of a game by each player and followed mechanically thereafter. Such plans are multistage contingency plans.

Thus every possible sequence of moves as represented by a path in the game tree is the joint result of the two strategies defined by that path.

Von Neumann and Morgenstern's argument was a short inductive statement. They observed that games of 0 moves whose initial position is terminal have an obvious strategy, the null strategy. They then pointed out that the first step of the strategy for a game of n moves is just to make that move that yields the highest value for the resulting game of $n - 1$ moves (as established by the use of the known optimal strategy that exists by the induction hypothesis).

They also proved that the value of a position always exists, and that minimaxing is the explicit method of computing it.

The basic principle of dynamic programming as formulated by Richard Bellman [Bel57] is another statement of the idea underlying minimaxing. (Here "programming" means *planning* or *decision-making*, not really *programming*.) Given a multistage decision process to be undertaken where one wishes to know a sequence of decisions that optimizes some desired quantity such as profit, the principle of dynamic programming is: select that decision that results in the state such that the subsequent use of an optimal policy from that state yields the fully optimal result. Thus to implement dynamic programming, we back up scores in the tree of decisions to find that sequence of decisions that optimizes the initial state. Often there are mathematical short-cut approaches to solving dynamic programming problems as opposed to brute force back up, but the objective is always to discover the optimizing path in the tree of decisions.

It is a remarkable fact that in a terminating two player perfect-information game where ties are not allowed, there must be a forced win for either the first or second player. That is: there exists a strategy for one player that guarantees that player will win, regardless of the opponent's actions. The proof of this fact is based on the valuation function scheme given above. The value $w(b)$ is 1 if and only if *box* has a forced win and -1 if and only if *circle* has a forced win, where b is the initial □ or ○ position.

We are interested not only in computing the maximum value to *box* of a position b, but also in discovering the particular move from position b, which eventually results in a terminal position from which that value is inherited.

The LISP function PICK takes a game position as an argument and computes the value of that position to *box* and the corresponding best successor position for the player to move as the two elements of the output dotted-pair. If there is no successor position to be recommended, then NIL is returned as the second element.

To use LISP, we must encode game positions as S-expressions. Such a game position S-expression includes, among other things, whether the position is a □ or a ○ position.

(PICK B) returns a dotted-pair $(x . m)$ where m is an optimal successor position for *box* of position B, and x is its score to *box*, where x and m are computed by minimaxing.

```
(SETQ PICK (LAMBDA (B)
                (COND ((DEEPENOUGH B) (CONS (U B) NIL))
                      (T (OPT (GENMOVES B)
                              (COND ((BOXPOS B) GREATERP)
                                    (T LESSP)))))))
```

(DEEPENOUGH B) returns T if $v[B]$ is a terminal position and NIL otherwise.

(BOXPOS B) returns T if $v[B]$ is a □ position and NIL if $v[B]$ is a ○ position.

(U B) returns the value -1, 0, or 1, which indicates the value to *box* of the terminal position $v[B]$.

(GENMOVES B) returns a list of all the successor positions of $v[B]$.
(W B) returns the minimaxed value to *box* of the position $v[B]$.

```
(SETQ W (LAMBDA (M) (CAR (PICK M))))
```

(OPT L P) returns a dotted-pair $(x . m)$ where x is a greatest score value among the scores of the positions in the list $v[L]$ if P = GREATERP, and x is a least score value among the scores of the positions in the list $v[L]$ if P = LESSP. In either case, m is a position that is an element of the list $v[L]$ whose score is x.

```
(SETQ OPT (LAMBDA (L P)
                  (COND ((EQ (CDR L) NIL) (CONS (W (CAR L)) (CAR L)))
                        (T (MB (CAR L) (W (CAR L)) (OPT (CDR L) P))))))

(SETQ MB (LAMBDA (A S Q)
                  (COND ((P S (CAR Q)) (CONS S A))
                        (T Q))))
```

> **Exercise 26.1:** Why isn't P an argument of MB? Hint: recall the discussion of *skip-binding*.

Now we have spelled out the machinery needed to program a great many games; namely, the functions PICK, W, OPT, and MB. The function PICK is the game-independent minimaxing program. The remaining required functions DEEPENOUGH, GENMOVES, U, and BOXPOS depend upon the game to be programmed and must be especially written for each game.

A major problem in using LISP to minimax a game tree is the requirement that an S-expression representation of game positions be devised and used. Such representations are generally large and complex and require complex functions to generate and valuate them. Often machine language or C permits a more compact and simple data structure to be used. (Consider, for example, defining a representation of a chess board, or even a checker board, "state".)

Another more fundamental problem is that simple minimaxing is too slow for all but small game trees. This forces us to abandon searching most game trees completely. Instead we shall search to a certain depth, and then *estimate* the values of the positions at which we stop. These estimates will then be backed up according to the minimaxing process. The estimated values will not be only –1, 0, and 1, but may be any real number in $[-1, 1]$ that serves as a score value of a position for *box*.

In order to evaluate a position when we cannot search ahead to terminal positions, we can introduce a valuation function s that can compute an estimate of the score of *any* position, including non-terminal positions. By convention, this score lies in $[-1, 1]$ and is always interpreted as being from the point of view of *box*. The function s is often called a *static valuation function* to emphasize its use in valuating a position without minimaxing.

The quality of the static valuation function can be critical, since valuation errors can occasionally be magnified rather than damped by minimaxing. Generally, a valuation function is defined as a real-valued function based on a collection of measurements or feature values that describe the position in question. Often a weighted linear combination of feature values is used. A more elaborate function that may take into account various dependencies between features can also be devised. Features can be concrete, such as "the relative piece advantage," or abstract, such as "center control." Abstract features must finally be defined in terms of concrete features. The selection of features is often difficult. The problem of having a program automatically discover (with intent) good features that "span" the description of a position is completely unsolved, although much interest in this and other related issues exists. (We say "with intent," because statistical methods like neural nets may provide a result that works, but is inexplicable in terms of discovered features.) Machine learning, as pioneered by Arthur Samuel, has generally meant adaptively modifying coefficients in the evaluation function so as to change its value to better describe positions that are known to be good or bad by other means. A program that truly learns a game, however, must learn features as well as coefficients.

We shall now consider an improved form of the minimax procedure known as the $\alpha\beta$ algorithm. A complete exposition of the $\alpha\beta$ algorithm is given by D.E. Knuth and R.W. Moore [KnuMo75].

The $\alpha\beta$ algorithm is based on the observation that if we have the situation

$$
\begin{array}{c}
1 \\
\swarrow \quad \downarrow \quad \searrow \\
1.1 \qquad 1.2 \qquad \cdots \\
\alpha \\
\swarrow \quad \downarrow \quad \searrow \\
1.2.1 \quad \cdots \quad 1.2.n \\
\beta
\end{array}
$$

where α is the value of position 1.1 and β is the value of position 1.2.1 with $\beta < \alpha$, and where position 1 is a □ position, then the score of position 1.2 will be at most β, which cannot compete with the value α to become the value of position 1, and hence we need not compute the scores of the nodes 1.2.2 through 1.2.n. A similar observation holds when $\beta > \alpha$ and node 1 is a ○ position. If these cut-off conditions are systematically tested for and taken advantage of in an appropriate modification of PICK, we have the $\alpha\beta$ algorithm.

> **Exercise 26.2:** Explain why the value of position 1.2 will be at most β.

LISP functions for the $\alpha\beta$ algorithm are given below. Note that skip-binding is extensively used. (Note: v denotes the LISP evaluation function as usual.)

(ABPICK B) returns a dotted-pair $(x . m)$ where m is an optimal successor position for *box* of position B, and x is its score to *box*, where x and m are computed with the $\alpha\beta$ algorithm.

```
(SETQ ABPICK (LAMBDA (B)
                (HPICK B (COND ((BOXPOS B) -1.1) (T 1.1)
                           (COND ((BOXPOS B) 1.1)
                                  (T -1.1))
                     0)))) )
```

(BOXPOS B) returns T if v[B] is a □ position and NIL if v[B] is a ○ position.

(HPICK B α β N) returns an optimal score-move dotted-pair $(x . m)$ where m is an optimal successor position for *box* of position v[B]. Position v[B] is at depth v[N] in the game tree being minimaxed. The arguments α and β are the □ and ○ $\alpha\beta$ cutoff values used to reduce the amount of work required.

```
(SETQ HPICK (LAMBDA (B ALPHA BETA N)
                    (COND ((DEEPENOUGH B N) (CONS (SCORE B) NIL))
                          (T (HOPT (GENMOVES B)
                                   (COND ((BOXPOS B) GREATERP) (T LESSP))
                                   BETA ALPHA (PLUS N 1))))))
```

(DEEPENOUGH B N) returns T if v[B] is a terminal position or is deemed to be deep enough in the game tree. Otherwise NIL is returned. v[N] is the depth of the position v[B] in the game tree.

(GENMOVES B) returns a list of all the successor positions of v[B].

(SCORE B) returns the estimated value to *box* of the position v[B]. It is the static valuation function.

(HOPT G P α β N) returns an optimal score-move dotted-pair $(x . m)$ where m is an optimal successor position in the list v[G] of a superior position, which is a □ position if v[P] = GREATERP and a ○ position if v[P] = LESSP. The list of successor positions v[G] is at depth v[N] in the game tree being heuristically minimaxed. The arguments α and β are the □ and ○ $\alpha\beta$ cutoff values used to reduce the amount of work required.

```
(SETQ HOPT (LAMBDA (G P ALPHA BETA N)
                   (OJ (CDR G) (HPICK (CAR G) ALPHA BETA N))))

(SETQ OJ (LAMBDA (G W)
                 (COND ((OR (P (CAR W) ALPHA) (NULL G)) W)
                       (T (OPTC (HOPT G P ALPHA (CAR W) N)))))) )
```

(OPTC Z) returns a score-move dotted-pair $(x . m)$, which is either the score-move pair v[W] or v[Z], or is such that x is a score value of one of the positions in the list v[D] and m is the corresponding successor position, which results in attaining that score. The score value x is a greatest score value if v[P] = GREATERP and x is a least score value of the positions in the list v[D] if v[P] = LESSP. In either case, m is a position that is an element of the list v[L] whose score is x.

```
(SETQ OPTC (LAMBDA (Z) (COND ((P (CAR W) (CAR Z)) W) (T Z))))
```

The $\alpha\beta$ algorithm may be elaborated in several ways to cope more effectively with complex games. However, as this is done, it becomes more difficult to express effectively in LISP.

The $\alpha\beta$ algorithm normally declares a position to be "good" if it is possible to follow a line of play from that position which results in a good position in the future. Because of uncertainty about the quality of the static valuation function, it may be safer to consider a position to be good if one can reach a number of good positions in the future. This may be approximated by giving a position a bonus if many of its successors are deemed to be bad for the opposing player. This device is discussed by Slagle and Dixon in [SlDi70]. Slagle [Sl63] gave the rather complicated logic needed to adapt the $\alpha\beta$ algorithm to handle this notion. In order to avoid such complexity, one can compute the bonus for a position based on the static scores of the successor positions as estimated by the static valuation function. This is relatively easy to incorporate into the usual $\alpha\beta$ algorithm.

It is also interesting to note that a move that leads to a position that has a poor score according to the static valuation function but has a dramatically improved score as a backed-up score from later resulting moves is a machine-discovered "trap" move. There may be some advantage to occasionally following such moves, depending, of course, on the reliability of the static valuation function. Active moves such as sacrifices are often trap moves.

Note that, generally, ABPICK will use less computation when we require that the list of successor positions produced by the GENMOVES function be ordered in sequence from best to worst positions with respect to the player to move. In this case, the very first move will have the score that is to be eventually backed up. This yields the maximum number of cutoffs in the course of considering such an ordered list of successor positions. Of course in practice we can only roughly approximate a perfect ordering and, as Knuth and Moore point out, a full ordering isn't really very useful anyway.

The GENMOVES function may also selectively omit some of the worst successor positions in order to avoid their consideration by the $\alpha\beta$ algorithm. Such *forward pruning* is not hazardless, but it is a virtual necessity in games such as chess in order to keep the growth of the game tree manageable. If detectable, similar positions to those already generated should be omitted. Similar positions may arise due to symmetry or other special circumstances.

It is possible to use the $\alpha\beta$ algorithm to search just a few levels in order to improve the scores used for ordering. This preliminary exploration is a special case of a more general idea called *dynamic ordering*, where we continually reorder successor position lists as the values of the positions are refined based on more information. In this case an entire game tree must be maintained whose subtrees can be rearranged as required. Even in the fixed-ordering case, it might be convenient to maintain an entire tree so as to reutilize the positions generated in the minimax searching. In fact, in a real game-playing situation, it is possible to use the subtree selected out of the current game tree by the opponent's move as the beginning game tree for the program's response. These elaborate full-tree schemes, particularly dynamic ordering, are of questionable use. Much depends upon the quality of the static valuation function being used.

Another difficult problem that requires a global consideration of the game tree is that of avoiding equivalent sequences of successive positions whose inclusion merely wastes time. Such equivalent sequences are often due to permutations of independent moves that produce the same final position. The $\alpha\beta$ algorithm will cut off some equivalent sequences, but not those that must be followed to establish initial backed up values.

An observation of interest is that the HPICK and GENMOVES functions could be reprogrammed in an appropriate language other than LISP to operate as *coroutines*, rather than the latter being a subroutine of the former. (A coroutine is effectively a "thread," that is, a procedure running conceptually in parallel with the main program with places within each coroutine where explicit coordinating communication [i.e., exchanging control between the two corountines] occurs.) In order to do this, we would define genmoves (b) to yield successively, in a common location, the various moves that produce the successors of b. Now when the next son of position b is needed in the course of minimaxing the game tree, the genmoves coroutine is restarted to compute the next move from where it left off within the current incarnation, or else a first move from b if no previous moves have been computed. The genmoves coroutine will signal when no more moves remain to be considered. Note that when a cut off occurs, we save the time and space of generating all the remaining moves that do not need to be examined. Of course, if genmoves secretly generates a complete list of moves, then this saving is illusory.

The question of when the $\alpha\beta$ algorithm has probed deeply enough in the game tree often depends upon the state of the game at the node we are at when the question is asked. In particular, if that position can be seen to be difficult to valuate statically, then it may pay to go deeper to resolve the difficulty. This is often the case when the position is one in a sequence of exchanges such as jump situations in checkers or piece exchanges in chess. Samuel calls such active positions *pitch* positions. The deepenough test may be that the level at which a position being considered is greater than a certain minimum and that the position in question is not a pitch position. The deepenough test may also depend upon the estimated quality of the positions on the path we are following. Moreover, time and space constraints should preferably be used in place of a simple depth criterion.

The problem of determining the savings gained by using the $\alpha\beta$ algorithm in place of simple minimaxing reduces to counting the number of nodes in a game tree of $d + 1$ levels that are visited during a typical $\alpha\beta$ search. For simplicity, we shall assume that every node has a constant branching factor f. Moreover we shall assume perfect ordering of successor positions by their scores, so that the maximum number of $\alpha\beta$ cut offs occur. Under these assumptions, the number of positions processed is:

$$(f+3)(1-f)^{\lceil d/2 \rceil}/(1-f) - (d+1) + 2(1 - d \bmod 2)f^{\lceil d/2 \rceil}.$$

Compared with the $(1-f)^{d+1}/(1-f)$ nodes visited with minimaxing, we can see that using the $\alpha\beta$ algorithm is roughly equivalent to reducing the branching factor of the game tree from f to $f^{1/2}$.

Detailed arguments that lead to the formula above are given by J.R. Slagle and J.K. Dixon [SlDi69]. A more realistic analysis is presented in [KnuMo75].

CHAPTER 27

■ ■ ■

The LISP Interpreter Program

The LISP interpreter presented below consists of three major subroutines: *sread*, *seval*, and *swrite*. The *sread* procedure reads input text, decomposes it into atom names and punctuation characters, enters all the new ordinary atoms and new number atoms that are encountered into the atom table and the number table, respectively, and constructs an S-expression representing the input. A typed-pointer to this S-expression is returned. If the input S-expression is not an atom, a corresponding list structure will be created in the list area. New ordinary atoms are entered in the atom table with the value: undefined.

The typed-pointer produced as output by *sread* is then passed as input to the *seval* subroutine. The procedure *seval* is the procedure that implements the LISP function EVAL. *seval* interpretively evaluates the S-expression pointed to by its input, calling itself recursively to evaluate subexpressions. The final result is an S-expression that is constructed in the list area if necessary, and a typed-pointer to this result S-expression is returned as output. If the input S-expression is illegal, *seval* prints an error message and goes to the point where *sread* is called to obtain more input. If the original input is evaluatable, the typed-pointer output from *seval* is provided as input to the *swrite* procedure. The *swrite* procedure assembles the names and punctuation characters needed to form a text string representing the given S-expression and prints this string at the terminal.

The entire LISP interpreter is thus of the following form.

1. Initialization steps
2. $i \leftarrow sread(\ )$
3. $j \leftarrow seval(i)$
4. $swrite(j)$
5. goto step 2.

We will present the explicit data structures and procedures that comprise much of a working LISP interpreter. It is common to present an interpreter function for LISP written in LISP as was done in the original LISP 1.5 manual [MIT62]. However, except for its pedagogical value, this is a sterile undertaking. In this book, the C programming language will be used.

It is important to note at this point that reading this program is the hardest thing in this little book that you might undertake. It is assumed that you are fluent in C, or will study independently to become so. And even then, there are, as in most substantial programs, places where the motivation of various statements may be obscure. Nevertheless, if you do read at least parts of this program, you will be rewarded by the

© Gary D. Knott 2017
G. D. Knott, *Interpreting LISP*, DOI 10.1007/978-1-4842-2707-7_27

minor, but cumulatively important, programming devices you encounter. (You may find that reading this program in small doses, revisiting procedures several times, just as you would if you were coding it, is a good approach.)

LISP in C

The following C program should run on any system where a C program can be compiled, although some minor fiddling may be needed to get it compiled in a specific environment. In particular, it runs on MS-DOS or within a DOS-window (command-line window) in MS-Windows, and on Unix/Linux from the command-line (i.e., in a terminal window).

The ASCII text files *lisp.c, linuxenv.h, Makefile*, and *lispinit* that you need to construct your own copy of this LISP Interpreter are downloadable from www.apress.com/lisp or from www.civilized.com.

In the C program below we use "publication notation"; specifically, we write ≤ for "<=" ≥ for ">=", ≠ for "!=", ≪ for "<<"; and in some comments, we write ← to denote the assignment operation, and we write = for "==" which is written "EQ" in our C-code via a macro-definition.

```
/* Filename: ~/lisp/lisp.c    Revision Date: Sept. 3, 1999 */
/* ================================================================= */
/* _____
   LISP INTERPRETER

   This progam is a GOVOL LISP interpreter. This interpreter consists of three major
   functions: SREAD, SEVAL, and SWRITE. SREAD scans the input string for input
   S-expressions (atoms and dotted pairs) and returns a corresponding typed-pointer. The
   SEVAL function takes as input a typed-pointer p to an input S-expression and evaluates
   it and returns a typed-pointer to its result. SWRITE takes as input the typed-pointer
   returned from SEVAL and prints out the result.

   LISP input lines beginning with a "/" are comment lines. Indirect input text is taken from
   a file Z to replace the directive of the form "@Z" in the input stream. SEVAL tracing can
   be turned on by using the directive "!trace", and turned off with the directive "!notrace".
   _____ */
/* ================================================================= */
```

/*Defining 8-, 16-, 32-, and 64-bit integers is tricky in C. Usually the definitions int8 = char, int16 = short int, and int32 = long int work for a compiler for C configured for a 32-bit CPU. For newer compilers that compile C configured for a 64-bit CPU, it is generally okay to use the defined types int16_t and int32_t given to us by typedefs in the header file types.h or in stdint.h, which is what we do here. */

```
#define int16 int16_t
#define int32 in32_t
```

/* We declare a forward function for any function used before it is defined. */
```
#define forward

#include "linuxenv.h"
```

/* The header file linuxenv.h declares strlen(), strcpy(), strcmp(), calloc(), fflush(), fopen(),
fclose(), fprintf(), sprintf(), fgetc(), labs(), floor(), and pow(). Also the type FILE is defined,
and the longjump register-save structure template: jmp buf is defined. The linuxenv.h include-
file includes the C header files that define these functions and data-object templates for a
Linux environment. In general, a similar environment header file will need to be constructed
by hand for each specific "platform" where this program is to be compiled and run. */

```
#define NULL 0L
#define EOF (-1)
#define EOS (0)

#define EQ ==
#define OR ||
#define AND &&
#define NOT !

#define n 1000        /* size of atom table and number table */
#define m 6000        /* size of list-area */
```
/* The values for n and m should be made much larger for a more-useful LISP interpreter.
    Also note n and m are not variables, they are constants substituting the symbols n and m.
    It is, of course, easy to change this, if you wish. */

```
jmp buf env;          /* struct to hold environment for longjump */
char *sout;           /* general output buffer pointer */
```

/* The atom table */
```
struct Atomtable {char name[16]; int32 L; int32 bl; int32 plist;} Atab[n];
```

/* The number table is used for storing floating point numbers. The field nlink is used for
    linking number table nodes on the number table free space list. */
```
union Numbertable {double num; int16 nlink;} Ntab[n];
```

/* the number hash index table */
```
int16 nx[n];
```

/* the number table free space list head pointer */
```
int16 nf=-1;
```

/* the number table mark array is used in garbage collection to mark number-table entries
    that are not to be returned to the free space list */
```
char nmark[n];  /* an array of 1-bit entries would suffice */
```

/* The list area */
```
struct Listarea {int32 car; int32 cdr;} *P;
```

/* the list area free space list head pointer */
```
int16 fp=-1;
```

```
/* the put-back variable */
int32 pb=0;

/* The input string and related pointers */
char *g,*pg,*pge;

/* the input stream stack structure and head pointer */
struct Insave {struct Insave *link; char *pg, *pge; char g[202]; FILE *filep;};
struct Insave *topInsave;

/* the input prompt character */
char prompt;

/* seval depth count and trace switch */
int16 ct=0, tracesw=0;

/* Global ordinary atom typed-pointers */
int32 nilptr,tptr,currentin,eaL,quoteptr,sk,traceptr;

/* number of free list-nodes */
int32 numf;

/* define global macros */

#define A(j)            P[j].car
#define B(j)            P[j].cdr
#define AL(j)           Atab[j].L
#define Abl(j)          Atab[j].bl

#define type(f)         (((f)>>28) & 0xf)
#define ptrv(f)         (0x0fffffff & (f))
#define sexp(t)         ((t) EQ 0 OR (t) EQ 8 OR (t) EQ 9)
#define fctform(t)      ((t)>9)
#define builtin(t)      ((t) EQ 10 OR (t) EQ 11)
#define userdefd(t)     ((t) EQ 12 OR (t) EQ 13)
#define dottedpair(t)   ((t) EQ 0)
#define fct(t)          ((t) EQ 10 OR (t) EQ 12 OR (t) EQ 14)
#define unnamedfsf(t)   ((t)>13)
#define namedfsf(t)     ((t)>9 AND (t)<14)
#define tp(t,j)         ((t) | (j))
#define ud(j)           (0x10000000 | (j))
#define se(j)           (0x00000000 | (j))
#define oa(j)           (0x80000000 | (j))
#define nu(j)           (0x90000000 | (j))
#define bf(j)           (0xa0000000 | (j))
#define bs(j)           (0xb0000000 | (j))
#define uf(j)           (0xc0000000 | (j))
#define us(j)           (0xd0000000 | (j))
#define tf(j)           (0xe0000000 | (j))
#define ts(j)           (0xf0000000 | (j))
```

```
/* variables used in file operations */
FILE *filep;
FILE *logfilep;
```

```
/* forward references (Look-up the SAIL Programming language to see the genesis of
'forward'). */
forward int32 seval(int32 i);
forward void initlisp(void);
forward int32 sread(void);
forward void swrite(int32 i);
forward int32 newloc(int32 x, int32 y);
forward int32 numatom (double r);
forward int32 ordatom (char *s);
forward void gc(void);
forward void gcmark(int32 p);
forward char getgchar(void);
forward char lookgchar(void);
forward void fillg(void);
forward int32 e(void);
forward void error(char *s);
forward int16 fgetline(char *s, int16 lim, FILE *stream);
forward void ourprint(char *s);
```

```
/* ================================================================= */
void main(void)
/* -----------------------------------------------------------------
```

   This is the main read/eval/print loop.

```
   ----------------------------------------------------------------- */
{initlisp();
 setjmp(env); /* calling error() returns to here by longjmp() */
 /* This is the main loop of the LISP interpreter. */
 for (;;) { ourprint("\n"); prompt='*'; swrite(seval(sread()));}
}
```

```
/* ================================================================= */
void error(char *msg)
/* -----------------------------------------------------------------
```

   *Type out the message in the string array msg and do a longjmp() to top level afterward to
   where setjmp was called.*

```
   ----------------------------------------------------------------- */
{int32 i,t;
```

```
 /* discard all input S-expression and argument list stacks */
 Atab[currentin].L=nilptr; Atab[eaL].L=nilptr; Atab[sk].L=nilptr;
 /* reset all atoms to their top-level values */
 for (i=0; i<n; i++) if ((t=Atab[i].bl)≠nilptr)
    {while (t≠nilptr) t=B(t); Atab[i].L=A(t); Atab[i].bl=nilptr;}
 ct=0; ourprint("::"); ourprint(msg); ourprint("\n");
 longjmp(env,-1);
}
```

```
/* ====================================================================== */
void ourprint(char *s)
/* char *s; message to be printed out and logged */
/* ---------------------------------------------------------------------
    Print the string s in the log file and on the terminal.
                                                                  ------ */
{printf("%s",s); fprintf(logfilep,"%s",s); fflush(logfilep);}


/* ====================================================================== */
void initlisp(void)
/* ---------------------------------------------------------------------
    This procedure installs all built-in functions and special forms into the atom table. It also
    initializes the number table and the list area.
                                                                  ------ */
{int32 i;

static char *BI[] =
    {"CAR","CDR","CONS","LAMBDA","SPECIAL","SETQ","ATOM","NUMBERP","QUOTE",
     "LIST","DO","COND","PLUS","TIMES","DIFFERENCE","QUOTIENT","POWER",
     "FLOOR","MINUS","LESSP","GREATERP","EVAL","EQ","AND","OR","SUM","PRODUCT",
     "PUTPLIST","GETPLIST","READ","PRINT","PRINTCR","MKATOM","BODY","RPLACA",
     "RPLACD","TSETQ", "NULL", "SET"
    };

static char BItype[] =
    {10,10,10,11,11,11,10,10,11,10,
     10,11,10,10,10,10,10,10,10,10,
     10,10,10,11,11,10,10,10,10,10,
     10,10,10,10,10,10,11,10,11
    };

/* number of built-ins in BI[~] and BItype[~] above */
#define NBI 39

/* allocate a global character array for messages */
sout=(char *)calloc(80,sizeof(char));

/* allocate the input string */
g=(char *)calloc(202,sizeof(char));

/* allocate the list area */
P=(struct Listarea *)calloc(m,sizeof(struct Listarea));

/* initialize atom table names and the number table */
  for (i=0; i<n; i++)
    {Atab[i].name[0]='\0'; nmark[i]=0; nx[i]=-1; Ntab[i].nlink=nf; nf=i;}
```

114

```
/* install typed-case numbers for builtin functions and and special forms into the
   atom table */
for (i=0; i<NBI; i++)
   {Atab[ptrv(ordatom(BI[i]))].L=tp(((((int32)BItype[i])≪28),(i+1));}


nilptr=ordatom("NIL"); Atab[ptrv(nilptr)].L=nilptr;
tptr=ordatom("T");      Atab[ptrv(tptr)].L=tptr;
quoteptr=ordatom("QUOTE");
```

/ Creating and using the list-valued atoms CURRENTIN, eaL, and sreadlist in the atom
   table is a means to ensure that we protect the list-nodes in these lists during garbage
   collection. This is one of a few "tricks" employed in this program. We make these atom
   names lowercased to keep them private. */*

```
currentin=ptrv(ordatom("currentin")); Atab[currentin].L=nilptr;
eaL=ptrv(ordatom("eaL")); Atab[eaL].L=nilptr;
sk=ptrv(ordatom("sreadlist")); Atab[sk].L=nilptr;

#define cilp Atab[currentin].L
#define eaLp Atab[eaL].L
#define skp Atab[sk].L
```

```
/** initialize the bindlist (bl) and plist fields */
for (i=0; i<n; i++) Atab[i].bl=Atab[i].plist=nilptr;
```

```
/* set up the list area free space list */
for (i=1; i<m; i++) {B(i)=fp; fp=i;} numf=m-1;
```

```
/* open the logfile */
logfilep=fopen("lisp.log","w");
ourprint("ENTERING THE GOVOL LISP INTERPRETER\n");
```

/ establish the input buffer g and the input stream stack topInsave and prepare to read-in
   predefined functions and special forms from the text file lispinit; these should include
   APPEND, REVERSE, EQUAL, APPLY, MEMBER, INTO, ONTO, NOT, ASSOC, NPROP,
   PUTPROP, GETPROP, and REMPROP. */*

```
topInsave=NULL;
strcpy(g,"@lispinit ");
pg=g; pge=g+strlen(g); /* initialize start & end pointers to the string g */
filep=stdin;
}
```

Exercise 27.1: Read ahead to learn how the loading of the input buffer string g with the text @lispinit causes the LISP functions in the file lispinit to be defined and write a definitive comment about this initialization process for inclusion in the code above.

```
/* ================================================================= */
int32 sread(void)
/* ---------------------------------------------------------------
```

This procedure scans an input string g using a lexical token scanning routine, e(), where e() returns

1 if the token is '('
2 if the token is "' (single-quote)
3 if the token is '.'
4 if the token is ')'

or a typed-pointer d to an atom or number stored in row ptrv(d) in the atom or number tables. Due to the typecode (8 or 9) of d, d is a negative 32-bit integer. The token found by e() is stripped from the front of g.

sread constructs an S-expression corresponding to the scanned input string and returns a typed-pointer to it as its result.

There is occasion to "put back" open parentheses and single quote symbols onto g within sread. This is done by loading the global putback variable, pb, which is interrogated and reset as appropriate within E.

```
 --------------------------------------------------------------- */

{int32 j,k,t,c;

if ((c=e())≤0) return(c);
if (c EQ 1) if ((k=e()) EQ 4) return(nilptr); else pb=k;
/* skp is defined as Atab[sk].L.*/
skp=newloc(nilptr,skp); /* push a new node on the skp list. */
A(skp)=j=k=newloc(nilptr,nilptr);

/* we will return k, but we will fill node j first. */
if (c EQ 1)
    {scan:   A(j)=sread();  /* read the first element. */
     next:   if ((c=e())≤2) {t=newloc(nilptr,nilptr); B(j)=t; j=t;
                             if (c≤0) {A(j)=c; goto next;}
                             pb=c; goto scan;
                            }
     if (c≠4) {B(j)=sread(); if (e()≠4) error("syntax error");}
     skp=B(skp); /* pop the skp list. */ return(k);
    }
```

```
  if (c EQ 2)
    {A(j)=quoteptr; B(j)=t=newloc(nilptr,nilptr); A(t)=sread();
     skp=B(skp); /* pop the skp list. */ return(k);
    }
  error("bad syntax");
}
```

Exercise 27.2: The *sread* procedure does not handle the NIL macro (). Propose a modification that does handle ().

Solution 27.2: Just before "$k \leftarrow newloc(nilptr, nilptr)$" insert "if $c = 1$ then if $(k \leftarrow E()) = 4$ then return(*nilptr*) else $pb \leftarrow k$". Another solution, which is adopted here, is to have the *E*-procedure recognize () and return *nilptr* when () is seen.

```
/* =============================================================== */
int32 e(void)
/* ---------------------------------------------------------------
```

E is a lexical token scanning routine which scans the chars in the input stream to extract the next token and returns

1 if the token is '('
2 if the token is "'
3 if the token is '.'
4 if the token is ')'

or a negative typed-pointer to an entry in the atom table or the the number table.
```
   ----------------------------------------------------------------- */
{double v,f,k,sign;
 int32 i,t,c;
 char nc[15], *np;
 struct Insave *tb;

#define OPENP  '('
#define CLOSEP ')'
#define BLANK  ' '
#define SINGLEQ "
#define DOT    '.'
#define PLUS   '+'
#define MINUS  '-'
#define CHVAL(c) (c-'0')
#define DIGIT(c) ('0'≤(c) AND (c)≤'9')
#define TOUPPER(c)  ((c) + 'A'-'a')
#define ISLOWER(c)  ((c)≥'a' AND (c)≤'z')

 if (pb≠0) {t=pb; pb=0; return(t);}

start:while ((c=getgchar()) EQ BLANK);   /* remove blanks */
```

```
if (c EQ OPENP)
   {while (lookgchar() EQ BLANK) getgchar(); /* remove blanks */
    if (lookgchar() EQ CLOSEP) {getgchar(); return(nilptr);} else return(1);
   }
if (c EQ EOS)
   {if (topInsave EQ NULL) {fclose(logfilep); exit(0);}
    /* restore the previous input stream */
    fclose(filep);
    strcpy(g,topInsave→g); pg=topInsave→pg; pge=topInsave→pge;
    filep=topInsave→filep; topInsave=topInsave→link;
    if (prompt EQ '@') prompt='>';
    goto start;
   }
if (c EQ SINGLEQ) return(2);
if (c EQ CLOSEP) return(4);
if (c EQ DOT)
   {if (DIGIT(lookgchar())) {sign=1.0; v=0.0; goto fraction;} return(3);}
if (NOT (DIGIT(c) OR ((c EQ PLUS OR c EQ MINUS) AND
      (DIGIT(lookgchar()) OR lookgchar() EQ DOT))))
   {np=nc; *np++=c;        /* put c in nc[0] */
    for (c=lookgchar();
           c≠BLANK AND c≠DOT AND c≠OPENP AND c≠CLOSEP;
           c=lookgchar())
        *(np++)=getgchar(); /* add a character */
    *np=EOS; /* nc is now a string */
    if (*nc EQ '@')
        {/* switch input streams */
         /* save the current input stream */
         tb=(struct Insave *)calloc(1,sizeof(struct Insave));
         tb→link=topInsave; topInsave=tb;
         strcpy(tb→g,g); tb→pg=pg; tb→pge=pge; tb→filep=filep;

         /* set up the new input stream */
         *g=EOS; pg=pge=g; prompt='@';
         filep=fopen(nc+1,"r"); /* skip over the @ */
         goto start;
        }
    /* convert the string nc to upper case */
    for (np=nc; *np≠EOS; np++)
        if (ISLOWER((int16)*np)) *np=(char)TOUPPER((int16)*np);
    return(ordatom(nc));  ⌐
   }
if (c EQ MINUS) {v=0.0; sign=-1.0;} else {v=CHVAL(c); sign=1.0;}
while (DIGIT(lookgchar())) v=10.0*v+CHVAL(getgchar());
if (lookgchar() EQ DOT)
   {getgchar();
    if (DIGIT(lookgchar()))
        {fraction:
         k=1.0; f=0.0;
         do {k=10.*k;f=10.*f+CHVAL(getgchar());} while (DIGIT(lookgchar()));
```

```
        v=v+f/k;
        }
    }
  return(numatom(sign*v));
}
```

Exercise 27.3: The procedure *e* does not handle LISP
input precisely as defined in this book. Describe the sins of
omission and commission occurring in *e*.

```
/* ================================================================== */
char getgchar(void)
/* --------------------------------------------------------------------
```
   Get a character from g.
```
   -------------------------------------------------------------------- */
{fillg(); return(*pg++);}


/* ================================================================== */
char lookgchar(void)
/* --------------------------------------------------------------------
```
   Look at the next character in g, but do not advance.
```
   -------------------------------------------------------------------- */
{fillg(); return(*pg);}


/* ================================================================== */
void fillg(void)
/* --------------------------------------------------------------------
```
   Read a line into g[ ]. A line starting with a "/" is a comment line to be discarded.
```
   -------------------------------------------------------------------- */
{while (pg≥pge)
    {sprompt:  if (filep EQ stdin) {sprintf(sout,"%c",prompt); ourprint(sout);}
    if (fgetline(g,200,filep)<0) return;
    if (filep EQ stdin) {fprintf(logfilep,"%s\n",g); fflush(logfilep);}
    if (*g EQ '/') goto sprompt;
    pg=g; pge=g+strlen(g); *pge++=' '; *pge='\0'; prompt='>';
    }
}


/* ================================================================== */
int16 fgetline(char *s, int16 lim, FILE *stream)
/* --------------------------------------------------------------------
```
   fgetline() gets a line (CRLF or just LF delimited) from stream and puts it into the string
   array (i.e., the buffer) s (up to lim chars). The function returns the length of this string.
   If there are no characters but just EOF, it returns -1 (EOF) as the length. There is no
   deblanking except to drop any CRs, and if present, the LF (\n). TABs are mapped to
   blanks.

Note when the file being read is stdin, an EOF will never be encountered, instead fgetc will wait until a complete line is typed, and then return the next character of that line until all the characters of that line have been consumed, whereupon fgetc blocks again, waiting for the next line.

```
---------------------------------------------------------------- */
{int16 c,i;
#define TAB 9
 for (i=0; i<lim AND (c=fgetc(stream))≠EOF AND c≠'\n'; ++i)
    {if (c EQ TAB) c=BLANK; s[i]=c;}
 s[i]='\0';
 if (c EQ EOF AND i EQ 0) return(-1); else return(i);
}
```

Exercise 27.4: The C function fgetc returns -1 (EOF) when it is called at the end of file. If fgetc is called again, it returns -1 again! We depend on this behavior here when an "indirect" file (such as the initialization file lispinit) is being read. Explain why this is.

Exercise 27.5: Note the function fillg loads the string g with a new input line. An additional blank character is added at the end of each line, except in certain circumstances having to do with reaching the end of file of an indirect file. Explain what the circumstances are where an additional final blank is not provided, and explain why generally, such a final blank is provided. Hint: think what might happen if such a blank were not interposed.

Exercise 27.6: This program assumes a stream of plain ASCII text is being provided as input, both from the keyboard and from any indirect file, however, this is not enforced. Should it be? And how can such enforcement be programmed?

```
/* ---------------------------------------------------------------
```
Now the routines numatom and ordatom are presented. The procedure gc which is called within numatom is the garbage-collector routine; garbage collection is an elegant concept that was popularized, if not introduced, by the first LISP interpreter. Understanding the somewhat subtle garbage-collection routines given below is central to understanding this LISP Interpreter program.

There are a number of subtle devices throughout the code given here, however, most of these are small, limited in scope, and fairly transparent with a little scrutiny. An exception is the use of a hash table storage and retrieval algorithm for maintaining the atom table and the number table. The basic idea is described next.

Suppose we are given a set of named items $a_1, a_2, \ldots, a_m$, that is, ordinary atoms, to be stored, and subsequently retrieved whenever desired. Each item has a unique name, which we may take to be a string of characters, and also a value, for example, some integer value. Thus each item is a name,value pair.

Let's establish an n-element table $T[0:n-1]$ with $n \geq m$. Each table entry is a structure with two components: name and value, and we write $T_i.name$ to specify the name field in T_i and $T_i.value$ to specify the value field in T_i. Further, we assume there is a code, for example, the null character 0, which does not appear as an item name and which can be used to indicate an empty T-element, for example, if $T_i.name = 0$ then T_i is unoccupied. We begin with $T_i.name$ initialized to 0 for $0 \leq i \leq n$.

Now to store an item a, we compute an "address" $j \in \{0, 1, \ldots, n-1\}$ where j depends on the string a.name. This address computation is called hashing, and the value j is called the hash value of the string a.name. (We expect the hash values of the items $a_1, a_2, \ldots, a_m$ to be well spread in the range of addresses $0, 1, 2, \ldots, n-1$; this is what makes hashing efficient. If the T-table entry T_j is unoccupied, then we store a in T_j, that is, we store a.name in $T_j.name$ and we store a.value in $T_j.value$. If the T-table entry T_j is occupied, we have a collision; in this case, we add one to j modulo n, that is, we set j to $(j+1) \mod n$, and go back to check if this adjacent T-table entry T_j is unoccupied, and if so, we store a in T_j. If we search the entire table in this manner then T is full and the item a cannot be stored. Otherwise we will store the item a in the first unoccupied entry encountered. This storage procedure is given below.

store(a) :

1. $j \leftarrow h(a.name)$. { Compute the hash function h on a.name. }
2. $f \leftarrow j$. { Remember the starting hash address in f. }
3. If (T_j is unoccupied) then ($T_j \leftarrow a$; return(1)).
4. $j \leftarrow (j+1) \mod n$.
5. If ($j = f$) then return(0). { '0' means T is full. }
6. Goto step 3.

To retrieve the item with the name α, we just follow the same sequence of probes in T until either we find a T-entry i with $T_i.name = \alpha$, or we find an unoccupied T-entry. In the former case, we have found the sought-for item; in the latter case, the sought-for item is not present. (We also have to account for the possiblilty that the entire table is full, although for efficiency we don't want to load the table more than about 90 percent full.) The retrieval procedure is:

retrieve(α):

1. $i \leftarrow h(a.name)$.
2. $f \leftarrow i$. { Remember the starting hash address in f. }
3. If (T_i is unoccupied) then return(-1). { '-1' means "not found". }
4. If ($T_i.name = \alpha$) then return(i). { i is the index such that $T_i.name = \alpha$. }
5. $i \leftarrow (i+1) \mod n$.
6. If ($j = f$) then return(-1) else goto step 3.

This scheme of probing in a random location to start finding a place to store an item or to start searching for an item, and just continuing the search at the next adjacent position if necessary is called open-addressing collision resolution.

Both the number table and the atom table are maintained as hash tables with open-addressing collision resolution. The number table is composed of the nx array, the Ntab array of (double num, int16 nlink) structures (where the double num field holds a 64-bit floating-point number), and the nmark array; it uses an indirect storage method in order to allow for unneeded number entries to be garbage collected.
-- */

```
/* ==================================================================== */
int32 numatom(double r)
/* -------------------------------------------------------------------
```
The number r is looked up in the number table and stored there as a lazy number atom if it is not already present. The typed-pointer to this number atom is returned.
--- */

```
{int32 j;
#define hashnum(r) ((*(1+(int32 *)(&r)) & 0x7fffffff) % n)
j=hashnum(r);
while (nx[j]≠-1)
    if (Ntab[nx[j]].num EQ r) {j=nx[j]; goto ret;} else if (++j EQ n) j=0;

/* Here nx[j] = -1; get an Ntab node to store a new number in. */
 if (nf<0) {gc(); if (nf<0) error("The number table is full");}
 nx[j]=nf; j=nf; nf=Ntab[nf].nlink; Ntab[j].num=r;
ret:  return(nu(j));
}
```

> **Exercise 27.7:** The number table is really represented here by the array *nx*. The entries in *nx* are either empty or are indices to *Ntab* elements, which are initially threaded on a free-space list. The 64-bit floating-point numbers are stored in the *num* field of the N tab entries. The reason for this is because we want to garbage collect the unneeded numbers in the number table from time to time and reuse the associated space. Can you find a way to reduce the space used for the number table while preserving both storage and retrieval efficiency and the ability for it to be garbage collected? Hint: can the num field and the nlink field in the Ntab entries be overlaid?

```
/* ==================================================================== */
int32 ordatom (char *s)
/* -------------------------------------------------------------------
```
The ordinary atom whose name is given as the argument string s is looked up in the atom table and stored there as an atom with the value undefined if it is not already present. The typed-pointer to this ordinary atom is then returned.
--- */

```
{int32 j,c;
#define hashname(s) (labs((s[0]≪16)+(s[(j=strlen(s))-1]≪8)+j) % n)

 j=hashname(s); c=j;
 while (Atab[j].name[0]≠EOS)
    {if (strcmp(Atab[j].name,s) EQ 0) goto ret;
     else if (++j EQ n) {j=0; if (j EQ c) error("atom table is full");}
    }

 strcpy(Atab[j].name,s); Atab[j].L=ud(j);
ret:  return(oa(j));
}
```

Exercise 27.8: Introduce a means so that *gc* will be called when the number table is about 90 percent full, rather than allowing the last 10 percent to be used before *gc* is called. Is there any point to doing this?

Exercise 27.9: If we were to abandon garbage collecting the number table, could we use a simple direct open-addressing hash table as we do with the atom table? Is there a 64-bit pattern that is not a possible floating-point number that we could use to indicate an *empty* location?

```
/* ================================================================ */
void swrite(int32 j)
/* ---------------------------------------------------------------- 

    The S-expression pointed to by the typed-pointer j is printed out.
   ---------------------------------------------------------------- */
{int32 i;
 int16 listsw;

 i=ptrv(j);
 switch (type(j))
    {case 0:  /* check for a list */
        j=i;
        while (type(B(j)) EQ 0) j=B(j);
        listsw=(B(j) EQ nilptr);
        ourprint("(");
        while (listsw)
           {swrite(A(i)); if ((i=B(i)) EQ nilptr) goto close; else ourprint(" ");}
        swrite(A(i)); ourprint(" . "); swrite(B(i));
close:   ourprint(")");
        break;

    case  8:  ourprint(Atab[i].name); break;
    case  9:  sprintf(sout,"%-g",Ntab[i].num); ourprint(sout); break;
    case 10:  sprintf(sout,"{builtin function: %s}",Atab[i].name);
```

```
                    ourprint(sout); break;
        case 11:    sprintf(sout,"{builtin special form: %s}",Atab[i].name);
                    ourprint(sout); break;
        case 12:    sprintf(sout,"{user defined function: %s}",Atab[i].name);
                    ourprint(sout); break;
        case 13:    sprintf(sout,"{user defined special form: %s}",Atab[i].name);
                    ourprint(sout); break;
        case 14:    ourprint("{unnamed function}"); break;
        case 15:    ourprint("{unnamed special form}"); break;
        }
}


/* ================================================================= */
void traceprint(int32 v, int16 osw)
/* int32 v; the object to be printed
 * int16 osw; 1 for seval() output, 0 for seval() input
 */
/* ---------------------------------------------------------------
   This function prints out the input and the result for each successive invocation of seval()
   when tracing is requested.
   ---------------------------------------------------------------- */
{if (tracesw>0)
    {if (osw EQ 1) sprintf(sout,"%d result:",ct--);
     else sprintf(sout,"%d seval:",++ct);
     ourprint(sout); swrite(v); ourprint("\n");
     }
}


/* ================================================================= */
int32 seval(int32 p)
/* ---------------------------------------------------------------
   Evaluate the S-expression pointed to by the typed-pointer p; construct the result value as
   necessary; return a typed-pointer to the result.
   ---------------------------------------------------------------- */

{int32 ty,t,v,f,fa,na;
 int32 *endeaL;
 static int32 j;
 static double s;
```

> **Exercise 27.10:** The local *static* variables j and s are essentially global variables that can only be accessed within seval; new instances of j and s are *not* established for each invocation of seval1, unlike the *recursive* variables ty, ty, t, v, f, fa, na, and *endeaL*. Can any of the recursive variables in seval be reclassified as static variables?

```
#define U1 A(p)
#define U2 A(B(p))
```

```
#define E1 A(p)
#define E2 A(B(p))
#define Return(v) {traceprint(v,1); return(v);}

 traceprint(p,0);
```

> **Exercise 27.11:** Explain the purpose of the function *traceprint*
> and the associated global variables *tracesw* and *ct*.

```
if(type(p)6=0)
   {
/* p does not point to a non-atomic S-expression.
```

If p is a type-8 typed-pointer to an ordinary atom whose value is a built-in or user-defined function or special form, then a typed-pointer to that atom-table entry with typecode 10, 11, 12, or 13, depending upon the value of the atom, is returned. Note that this permits us to know the names of functions and special forms.

If p is a type-8 typed-pointer to an ordinary atom whose value is not a built-in or user-defined function or special form, and thus has the typecode 8, 9, 14, or 15, then a typed-pointer corresponding to the value of this atom is returned.

If p is a non-type-8 typed-pointer to a number atom or to a function or special form (named or unnamed), then the same pointer p is returned. */

```
   if ((t=type(p))≠8) Return(p); j=ptrv(p);
```

/* *The association list is implemented with shallow binding in the atom table, so the current values of all atoms are found in the atom table.* */

```
   if (Atab[j].name[0] EQ '!')
      {tracesw=(strcmp(Atab[j].name,"!TRACE") EQ 0)?1:0; longjmp(env,-1);}

   if ((t=type(Atab[j].L)) EQ 1)
      {sprintf(sout,"%s is undefined\n",Atab[j].name); error(sout);}

   if (namedfsf(t)) Return(tp(t*28,j));
   Return(Atab[j].L);
   } /* end of if (type(p)≠0) */
```

> **Exercise 27.12:** What are the pros and cons of replacing
> the statement return(L_j) in the compound statement just
> above with the statement: if $L_j = p$ and *bindlist$_j$* $\neq$ *nilptr* then
> return($A[bindlist_j]$) else return(L_j)? Hint: think about evaluating
> (F G) where F and G are defined by (SETQ F (SPECIAL (G)
> ((EVAL G) 1))) and (SETQ G (LAMBDA (F) (PLUS F F))).

/* Save the list p consisting of the current function and the supplied arguments as the top
    value of the currentin list of lists to protect it from garbage collection. The currentin list is
    a list of lists. */

```
cilp=newloc(p,cilp);
```

/* compute the function or special form to be applied */
```
tracesw-- ; f=seval(A(p)); tracesw++; ty=type(f);
if (NOT fctform(ty)) error(" invalid function or special form");
f=ptrv(f); if (NOT unnamedfsf(ty)) f=ptrv(Atab[f].L);
```

/* now let go of the supplied input function */
```
A(cilp)=p=B(p);
```

/* If f is a function (not a special form), build a new list of its evaluated arguments and add
    it to the eaL list of lists. Then let go of the list of supplied arguments, replacing it with the
    new list of evaluated arguments. */
```
if (fct(ty))
   {/* compute the actual arguments */
     eaLp=newloc(nilptr,eaLp);
     /* evaluate the actual arguments and build a list by tail-cons-ing! */
     endeaL=&A(eaLp);
     while (p≠nilptr)
         {*endeaL=newloc(seval(A(p)),nilptr); endeaL=&B(*endeaL); p=B(p);}
     /* Set p to be the first node in the evaluated arguments list. */
     p=A(eaLp);
```

> **Exercise 27.13:** Expand &B(*endeaL) and explain the
> assignment statement endeaL = &B(*endeaL).

/* Throw away the current supplied arguments list by popping the curentin list. */
```
     cilp=B(cilp);
     }
```

/* At this point p points to the first node of the actual argument list. If p EQ nilptr, we have a
    function or special form with no arguments. */

```
if (NOT builtin(ty))
    {/* f is a non-builtin function or non-builtin special form.   do shallow binding of
     the arguments and evaluate the body of f by calling seval */
     fa=A(f); /* fa points to the first node of the formal argument list */
     na=0;     /* na counts the number of arguments */
```

/* run through the arguments and place them as the top values of the formal argument
    atoms in the atom table. Push the old value of each formal argument on its binding list. */
```
     if (type(fa) EQ 8 AND fa ≠ nilptr)
       {t=ptrv(fa); Atab[t].bl=newloc(Atab[t].L,Atab[t].bl);
        Atab[t].L=p; goto apply;}
```

```
    else
        while (p≠nilptr AND dottedpair(type(fa)))
            {t=ptrv(A(fa)); fa=B(fa);
             Atab[t].bl=newloc(Atab[t].L,Atab[t].bl);
             v=A(p); if (namedfsf(type(v))) v=Atab[ptrv(v)].L;
             Atab[t].L=v; ++na; p=B(p);
             }

if (p≠nilptr) error("too many actual arguments");
```

Exercise 27.14: Why did we need to build the *eaL* list, rather than just directly place each *seval* result as the new value of the corresponding formal argument?

Solution 27.14: To make sure that the successive formal argument bindings don't effect the evaluation of succeeding actual arguments which happen, directly or indirectly, to involve free variables whose names are also used within the current list of formal arguments, the rebinding of all formal arguments is delayed until all the actual arguments have been evaluated.

*/*The following code would forbid some useful trickery.*
*if (fa≠nilptr) error("too many formal argumentss"); */*

```
    /* now apply the non-builtin special form or function */
apply: v=seval(B(f));

    /* now unbind the actual arguments */
    fa=A(f);
    if (type(fa) EQ 8 AND fa ≠ nilptr)
        {t=ptrv(fa); Atab[t].L=A(Atab[t].bl); Atab[t].bl=B(Atab[t].bl);}
    else
        while (na-->0)
            {t=ptrv(A(fa)); fa=B(fa);
             Atab[t].L=A(Atab[t].bl); Atab[t].bl=B(Atab[t].bl);
             }
    } /* end non-builtins */
else
    { /* At this point we have a built-in function or special form. f is the pointer value of the
         atom in the atom table for the called function or special form and p is the pointer to
         the argument list.*/
    v=nilptr;
    switch (f) /* begin builtins */
    {case 1:     /* CAR */
        if (NOT dottedpair(type(E1))) error("illegal CAR argument");
        v=A(E1); break;
    case 2:      /* CDR */
        if (NOT dottedpair(type(E1))) error("illegal CDR argument");
        v=B(E1); break;
    case 3:      /* CONS */
```

```
   if (sexp(type(E1)) AND sexp(type(E2))) v=newloc(E1,E2);
   else error("Illegal CONS arguments");
   break;
```

/ for LAMBDA and SPECIAL, we could check that U1 is either an ordinary atom
or a list of ordinary atoms. */*

```
case 4:/* LAMBDA */ v=tf(newloc(U1,U2)); break;

case 5:/* SPECIAL */ v=ts(newloc(U1,U2)); break;
case 6:/* SETQ */
   f=U1; if (type(f)≠8) error("illegal assignment");
   assign:  v=ptrv(f); endeaL=&AL(v);
   doit: t=seval(U2);
   switch (type(t))
      {case 0:     /* dotted pair */
       case 8:     /* ordinary atom */
       case 9:     /* number atom */
          *endeaL=t; break;
       case 10:    /* builtin function */
       case 11:    /* builtin special form */
       case 12:    /* user-defined function */
       case 13:    /* user-defined special form */
          *endeaL=Atab[ptrv(t)].L;  break;
       case 14:    /* unnamed function */
          *endeaL=uf(ptrv(t)); break;
       case 15:    /* unamed special form */
          *endeaL=us(ptrv(t)); break;
      } /* end of type(t) switch cases */

   tracesw--; v=seval(f); tracesw++; break;
```

Exercise 27.15: Explain why a case above for *type*(t)=1 is not
necessary.

```
case 7:  /* ATOM */
   if ((type(E1)) EQ 8 OR (type(E1)) EQ 9) v=tptr; break;

case 8:  /* NUMBERP */
   if (type(E1) EQ 9) v=tptr; break;

case 9:  /* QUOTE */ v=U1; break;
case 10:  /* LIST */ v=p; break;
case 11:  /* DO */ while (p≠nilptr) {v=A(p); p=B(p);} break;

case 12:  /* COND */
   while (p≠nilptr)
```

```
        {t=A(p);
         if (seval(A(t))≠nilptr) {v=seval(A(B(t))); break;} else p=B(p);
         }
      break;

case 13:  /* PLUS */
    v=numatom(Ntab[ptrv(E1)].num+Ntab[ptrv(E2)].num); break;

case 14:  /* TIMES */
    v=numatom(Ntab[ptrv(E1)].num*Ntab[ptrv(E2)].num);  break;

case 15:  /* DIFFERENCE*/
    v=numatom(Ntab[ptrv(E1)].num-Ntab[ptrv(E2)].num); break;

case 16:  /* QUOTIENT */
    v=numatom(Ntab[ptrv(E1)].num/Ntab[ptrv(E2)].num); break;

case 17:  /* POWER */
    v=numatom(pow(Ntab[ptrv(E1)].num,Ntab[ptrv(E2)].num)); break;

case 18:  /* FLOOR*/ v=numatom(floor(Ntab[ptrv(E1)].num)); break;
case 19:  /* MINUS*/ v=numatom(-Ntab[ptrv(E1)].num); break;
case 20:  /* LESSP*/
    if(Ntab[ptrv(E1)].num<Ntab[ptrv(E2)].num) v=tptr; break;

case 21:  /* GREATERP*/
    if (Ntab[ptrv(E1)].num>Ntab[ptrv(E2)].num) v=tptr; break;

case 22:  /* EVAL*/ v=seval(E1); break;
case 23:  /* EQ*/ v=(E1 EQ E2)?tptr:nilptr; break;

case 24:  /* AND*/
    while (p≠nilptr AND seval(A(p))≠nilptr) p=B(p);
    if (p EQ nilptr) v=tptr;     /* else v remains nilptr */
    break;

case 25:  /* OR*/
    while (p≠nilptr AND seval(A(p)) EQ nilptr) p=B(p);
    if (p≠nilptr) v=tptr;        /* else v remains nilptr */
    break;

case 26:  /* SUM*/
    for (s=0.0; p≠nilptr; s=s+Ntab[ptrv(A(p))].num, p=B(p));
    v=numatom(s); break;

case 27:  /* PRODUCT*/
    for (s=1.0; p≠nilptr; s=s*Ntab[ptrv(A(p))].num, p=B(p));
    v=numatom(s); break;
```

```
case 28:  /* PUTPLIST */ v=E1; Atab[ptrv(v)].plist=E2; break;
case 29:  /* GETPLIST */ v=Atab[ptrv(E1)].plist; break;
case 30:  /* READ */ ourprint("\n>"); prompt=EOS; v=sread(); break;

case 31: /* PRINT */
   if (p EQ nilptr) ourprint(" ");
   else while (p≠nilptr) {swrite(A(p)); ourprint(" "); p=B(p);}
   break;

case 32:  /* PRINTCR */
   if (p EQ nilptr) ourprint("\n");
   else while (p≠nilptr) {swrite(A(p)); ourprint("\n"); p=B(p);}
   break;

case 33:  /* MKATOM */
   strcpy(sout,Atab[ptrv(E1)].name); strcat(sout,Atab[ptrv(E2)].name);
   v=ordatom(sout); break;

case 34:  /* BODY */
   if (unnamedfsf(type(E1))) v=ptrv(E1);
   else if (userdefd(type(E1))) v=ptrv(Atab[ptrv(E1)].L);
   else error("illegal BODY argument");
   break;

case 35:  /* RPLACA */
   v=E1;
   if (NOT dottedpair(type(v))) error("illegal RPLACA argument");
   A(v)=E2; break;

case 36:  /* RPLACD */
   v=E1;
   if (NOT dottedpair(type(v))) error("illegal RPLACD argument");
   B(v)=E2; break;

case 37:  /* TSETQ */
   if (Abl(f=ptrv(U1)) EQ nilptr) goto assign;
   v=Abl(f); while (B(v)≠nilptr) v=B(v);
   endeaL=&A(v); goto doit;

case 38:  /* NULL */
   if (E1 EQ nilptr) v=tptr; break;

case 39:  /* SET */
   f=seval(U1); goto assign;

default:  error("dryrot: bad builtin case number");
} /* end of switch cases */
```

```
} /* end builtins */
/* pop the eaL list or pop the currentin list, whichever is active */
if (fct(ty)) eaLp=B(eaLp); else cilp=B(cilp);

Return(v);
}
```

Exercise 27.16: What does the built-in special form TSETQ given in the code above do?

Exercise 27.17: Would it be a good idea if the "cond" case were rewritten as follows?

case 12: /* *cond* */ *while* $p \neq nilptr$ do if $(v \leftarrow seval(A[t \leftarrow A_p])) \neq nilptr$ then {if $B_t \neq nilptr$ then $v \leftarrow seval(A[B_t])$; break} else $p \leftarrow B_p$};

Exercise 27.18: Modify the "cond" case to make the final "else" option not require a T predicate; (COND $(P_1 R_1) \cdots (P_k R_k) R_{k+1})$ is to be interpreted as (COND $(P_1 R_1) \cdots (P_k R_k)$ (T R_{k+1})).

Exercise 27.19: If there are unexpectedly a few actual arguments provided for a built-in function or special form, this program may fail catastrophically. Suggest an approach to detect this type of error and prevent any failure. What happens if too many arguments are given?

Exercise 27.20: Modify the built-in function READ to take an optional file name argument, and to read its input from this file when specified.

Exercise 27.21: Functions and special forms are not included in the class of atoms, and thus cannot appear in dotted-pairs (although their ordinary-atom names can). There is an exception to this statement. What is it? Could the class of atoms be enlarged to include functions? Should it be?

Exercise 27.22: To add a new *builtin* function or special form to the LISP interpreter given above, we must first insert the *name* of the new function or special form at the end of the *BI array in the *initlisp* subroutine, and add its typecode (10 for a function and 11 for a special form) at the end of the "parallel" array BItype in the *initlisp* subroutine. The position i of an entry in the *BI and BItype arrays determines the *case number* to be used for the new function or special form to be $i + 1$. (Read the code in *lispinit* to see why that is.) Thus adding the new function or special form at the end of the *BI array means we need only add the next sequential case into the central switch statement in the *seval* subroutine as the case where the code for the new function or special form is placed.

Define a new built-in function named TYPECODE which returns the number typecode of its argument. Explain how this can be used to write LISP functions that check their arguments and issue error reports when necessary.

Exercise 27.23: The built-in special form LABEL is not handled. Provide code to implement LABEL. Hint: just place the typed-pointer of the λ-expression in the value field of the label variable to prepare for setting up to jump to APPLY.

Exercise 27.24: Often lists are used as one-dimensional arrays. In order to access the *i*-th element, a function called ACCESS may be defined. For example, with:

```
(SETQ ACCESS (LAMBDA (L I)
                    (COND ((EQ I 1) (CAR L))
                          (T (ACCESS (CDR L) (PLUS I -1)))))).
```

this function is often painfully slow. Add iterative code to make ACCESS a built-in function.

Exercise 27.25: Most versions of LISP provide the potentially-infinite class of functions CAAR, *CADR*, CDAR, CDDR, CAAAR, ... , where the interior A and D letters in the name of such a function specify that a corresponding sequence of CAR and CDR applications is to be done to the argument S-expression. Modify the program given here to provide for this class of functions.

Exercise 27.26: It is easy to write (MINUS N 1) when we mean (DIFFERENCE N 1). Suppose $v[N] = 4$. What output do we get when (MINUS N 1) is entered? Hint: set tracing on with the directive !trace and then enter (SETQ N 4) and (MINUS N 1).

Exercise 27.27: Many of the sections of code for built-in functions and special forms given above do not adequately check their arguments. In each such case, propose suitable error-checking code so that the LISP interpreter cannot directly or indirectly crash due to such incorrect input. Try to maintain whatever readability is currently present, since readability is a virtue equally as important as efficiency.

Exercise 27.28: Why isn't it a good idea to make REVERSE explicitly built in with the following code?

$\{$int32 $i, j, t; i \leftarrow E1; j \leftarrow B_i; B_i \leftarrow nilptr;$
while $j \neq nilptr$ do $\{t \leftarrow B_j; B_j \leftarrow i; i \leftarrow j; j \leftarrow t\}; v \leftarrow i\}.$

Exercise 27.29: There is code given in the program above that implements a built-in special form called TSETQ. Explain what TSETQ does.

Exercise 27.30: Define a new built-in function called PEVAL which takes an ordinary atom A as input and returns the previous pushed-down value of A at the head of the *bindlist* of A. What should you return if there is no such pushed-down value?

Exercise 27.31: Define an extension to LISP to handle the class of strings of characters as a datatype. In particular, let strings of characters be a class of legal LISP values, just as numbers, functions, and S-expressions are. What about a typecode for strings? Explain how strings might be stored. (Hint: use self-referential ordinary atoms.) How are constant strings written? Define the functions that provide for string manipulation. Include (CAT a b), (STRLEN a), and (SUBSTR a i j). Would STR, where $v[(STR x)] =$ the string of $v[x]$, be useful? What about introducing an inverse to STR? Define (READSTR) in a useful way. How will PRINT and PRINTCR handle strings? Can READ be redefined to optionally apply to a string? Are there other potentially useful new functions and extensions of old functions that are of interest? Strike a synthetic balance between utility and complexity.

```
/* ================================================================= */
int32 newloc(int32 x, int32 y)
/* -----------------------------------------------------------------
```
   Allocates and loads the fields of a new location in the list area. The car field is set to X
   and the cdr field is set to Y. The index of the new location is returned.
```
   ----------------------------------------------------------------- */
{int32 j;
  if (fp<0) {gcmark(x); gcmark(y); gc(); if (fp<0) error("out of space");}
  j=fp; fp=B(j); A(j)=x; B(j)=y; numf--; return(j);
}
```

Exercise 27.32: How does one "exit" from the LISP Interpreter given above?

Exercise 27.33: Reprogram the LISP interpreter given here to solve the problem that strings are not automatically allocated or automatically garbage collected in C by building a collection of string-handling toolkit procedures. Hint: arrange for all strings to live in a special garbage-collected area established especially for strings.

Exercise 27.34: Write the code for a new LISP function DEL which removes its atom argument x from the atom table. What will happen if the atom argument x is referred to in an S-expression?

Exercise 27.35: In the LISP interpreter above, indirect input is read from the file F when the directive @F is input. (Is this latter "input" a noun or a verb?) Although any output due to such indirect input is output to the screen and to the log file *lisp.log*, the contents of F itself are not printed on the screen nor are they entered in *lisp.log*. Modify the LISP Interpreter program to test for the value of an ordinary atom ECHOSW, and if ECHOSW does not exist or $v[\text{ECHOSW}] \notin \{1, 2, 3\}$, leave the output as it is currently done, while if $v[\text{ECHOSW}] = 1$ or $v[\text{ECHOSW}] = 3$, print the contents of each indirect file on the screen as it is read, and if $v[\text{ECHOSW}] = 2$ or $v[\text{ECHOSW}] = 3$, write the contents of each indirect file in the log file as it is read.

Exercise 27.36: Note that an input line beginning with '/' is a comment. (Try entering "/acomment". Also try entering "/notacomment".) The LISP Interpreter program above prompts for an input by printing the symbol *, and if the entered line is not a sequence of one or more complete S-expressions, then continuation input is prompted by printing ¿. In the special case where the input line given in response to * is empty, that is, the enter key is immediately hit, a > is printed to prompt for more input. Is this a rational design decision? Modify the LISP Interpreter program to prompt for further input in this special case with a *.

CHAPTER 28

■ ■ ■

Garbage Collection

As input S-expressions are provided to the LISP interpreter to evaluate, various list structures in the list area are constructed, both from the input and during the process of evaluation. Many of these list structures have no use after they have been initially used. Such useless data objects are called *garbage* data objects. In the case of list area nodes, a node is garbage if it cannot be reached. This means that it is not a node in any list structure that is the value of an ordinary atom, including user-defined function and special form values, nor is it reachable from any pushed-down values held in a *bindlist* list, nor does it occur within any property lists.

We need to find such useless list nodes and put them on the list-area free-space list so they may be reused; otherwise we will run out of list area memory on all but modest computations. This process is called *garbage collection*. A procedure for performing garbage collection called *gc* is described below.

Useless garbage entries also accumulate in the number table as input numbers, and computed numbers are created and become useless. The *gc* procedure also collects the garbage entries in the number table and makes them available for reuse. The *gc* procedure is only invoked when the list area is exhausted or when the number table cannot hold more numbers. In particular the *gc* procedure is called from within the *newloc* procedure given above whenever it is discovered that no list nodes are available.

> **Exercise 28.1:** Enumerate all the places in the LISP interpreter where the *gc* procedure is called.

> **Exercise 28.2:** One of the central routines that must permit garbage collection to occur at several points within itself is the *sread* procedure. Study the *sread* procedure and explain in detail how and why it works.

Below we give the garbage-collection function {\tt gc} and the ancillary routine {\tt gcmark} which implement the garbage-collection "service" used in the LISP Interpreter program.

© Gary D. Knott 2017
G. D. Knott, *Interpreting LISP*, DOI 10.1007/978-1-4842-2707-7_28

```
/* ================================================================ */
void gc(void)
/* ----------------------------------------------------------------
```

    Garbage collector for the number table and the listarea.
```
    ---------------------------------------------------------------- */
{int32 i,t;
#define marked(p)    ((A(p) & 0x08000000)6=0)
#define unmark(p)    (A(p) &= 0xf7ffffff)
```

/* *Mark everything reachable from the atom table.* */
```
  for (i=0; i<n; i++)
    {gcmark(Atab[i].L); gcmark(Atab[i].bl); gcmark(Atab[i].plist);}
```

/* *gcmark has set nmark[i] =1 for every number Ntab[i].num reachable from the atom table or from a list-node. Now we garbage-collect the number table by re-storing every reachable number, and claiming the rest for reuse.* */
```
for (i=0; i<n; i++) nx[i]=-1;

for (nf=-1,i=0; i<n; i++)
   if (nmark[i] EQ 0) {Ntab[i].nlink=nf; nf=i;}
   else /* restore num[i] */
       {t=hashnum(Ntab[i].num);
         while (nx[t]6=-1) if ((++t) EQ n) t=0;
         nx[t]=i; nmark[i]=0;
         }
```

  /* *build the new list-node free-space list and return.* */
```
  fp=-1; numf=0;
  for (i=1; i<m; i++) if (NOT marked(i)) {B(i)=fp; fp=i; numf++} else unmark(i);
}
```

```
/* ================================================================ */
void gcmark(int32 p)
/* ----------------------------------------------------------------
```

    Mark the object, possibly a sub-tree, specified by p. At the same time, for every number pointer referencing Ntab[i] encountered, set nmark[i] =1 to mark Ntab[i].num as a "reachable" number to be preserved.
```
    ---------------------------------------------------------------- */
{static int32 s,t;
#define marknode(p)  (A(p) |= 0x08000000)
#define marknum(t,p)  if ((t) EQ 9) nmark[ptrv(p)]=1
#define listp(t)      ((t) EQ 0 OR (t)>11)
```

```
start:
 t=type(p);
 if (listp(t))
    {p=ptrv(p); if (marked(p)) return; t=A(p); marknode(p);
     if (NOT listp(type(t))) {marknum(type(t),t); p=B(p); goto start;}
     s=B(p); if (NOT listp(type(s))) {marknum(type(s),s); p=t; goto start;}
     gcmark(t);        /* recursive call to mark the subtree A(p). */
     p=B(p); goto start; /* equivalent to gcmark(B(p)) */
    }
 else marknum(t,p);
}
```

Exercise 28.3: Why don't we have a scheme for "marking" the entries in the atom table found while traversing S-expressions?

Here is an indirect file that defines the function mg that can be used to generate a bunch of "disconnected" list nodes that will eventually force garbage collection to occur. We can use this function to superficially test garbage collection.

/ file:gctest to define mg for testing garbage collection.

```
(SETQ DONE 'DONE)

(SETQ MG (LAMBDA (N) (COND ((GREATERP 0 (SETQ N (DIFFERENCE N 1))) DONE)
                          ((EQ 1 (CONS (CONS N T) (CONS NIL T))) 7)
                          ( T (MG N)) ) ) )
```

/ type (mg 700) or a similar command to force garbage-collection.

Exercise 28.4: Create the above file in your lisp directory with the name gctest. Then run the LISP Interpreter program and enter the directive @gctest. Then enter (mg 500). Then enter (mg 700). Then enter (mg 990). Then enter (mg 1000). Explain what you see.

Exercise 28.5: Can you devise a way to discard unneeded ordinary atoms and thus reclaim space in the atom table for reuse? Hint: first try to handle those unreferenced ordinary atoms whose values are undefined.

Exercise 28.6: Can you cause *gc* to loop forever by building a circular list using RPLACA and/or RPLACD?

Exercise 28.7: Are there any bugs in the LISP interpreter program given here?

Solution 28.7: Indubitably! For example, try entering an illegal or non-existent indirect input file name: for example, @ ABC where the file ABC does not exist. And try entering just @. (You should, of course, fix all these bugs in your own copy of the LISP interpreter !-).)

/ end of file lisp.c */*

■ ■ ■

## CHAPTER 29

The *lispinit* File, the *linuxenv.h* File, and the *Makefile* File

Below is the *lispinit* file used by the LISP Interpreter program. This text file contains the definitions of various LISP functions that are part of GOVOL LISP, but which are provided by just "reading" them from this file and establishing them by executing the SETQ expressions given herein rather than hard-coding them into the LISP Interpreter.

```
/filename: ~/lisp/lispinit           revision date: October 15, 1988

(SETQ APPEND (LAMBDA (X Y) (COND ((EQ X NIL) Y)
   ((ATOM X) (CONS X Y))
   (T (CONS (CAR X) (APPEND (CDR X) Y)) )) ))

(SETQ REVERSE (LAMBDA (X) (COND ((ATOM X) X)
   (T (APPEND (REVERSE (CDR X)) (CONS (CAR X) NIL )))) ))

(SETQ EQUAL (LAMBDA (X Y) (COND ((OR (ATOM X) (ATOM Y)) (EQ X Y))
   ((EQUAL (CAR X) (CAR Y)) (EQUAL (CDR X) (CDR Y)))
   (T NIL)) ))

(SETQ NOT NULL)

(SETQ ZEROP (LAMBDA (X) (COND ((EQ X 0) T))))

(SETQ MEMBER (LAMBDA (A S) (COND ((EQ S NIL) NIL) ((EQUAL A (CAR S)) T)
(T (MEMBER A (CDR S))) )))

(SETQ INTO (LAMBDA (G L) (COND ((NULL L) L) (T (CONS (G (CAR L))
(INTO G (CDR L))))))) 

(SETQ ONTO (LAMBDA (G L) (COND ((NULL L) L) (T (CONS (G L)
(ONTO G (CDR L)))))))
```

© Gary D. Knott 2017
G. D. Knott, *Interpreting LISP*, DOI 10.1007/978-1-4842-2707-7_29

```
(SETQ APPLY (SPECIAL ($G $X) (EVAL (CONS $G $X))))

(SETQ SORT (LAMBDA (X)
   (COND ((NULL X) X) (T (MERGE (CAR X) (SORT (CDR X)))))))

(SETQ MERGE (LAMBDA (V L) (COND ((OR (NULL L) (LESSP V (CAR L))) (CONS V L))
   (T (CONS (CAR L) (MERGE V (CDR L)))))))

(SETQ GETPROP (LAMBDA (A P) (ASSOC (GETPLIST A) P)))

(SETQ ASSOC (LAMBDA (L P) (COND ((NULL L) NIL)
   (T (COND ((EQUAL P (CAR (CAR L))) (CDR (CAR L)))
   (T (ASSOC (CDR L) P)))))))

(SETQ PUTPROP (LAMBDA (A P W) (PUTPLIST A
   (CONS (CONS P W) (GETPLIST (REMPROP A P W))))))

(SETQ REMPROP (LAMBDA (A P W) (PUTPLIST A (NAX (GETPLIST A) (CONS P W)))))

(SETQ NAX (LAMBDA (L P) (COND
   ((NULL L) NIL) ((EQUAL (CAR L) P) (CDR L))
   (T (DO (NX L P) L)))))

(SETQ NX (LAMBDA (L P) (COND ((NULL (CDR L)) NIL)
   ((EQUAL P (CAR (CDR L))) (RPLACD L (CDR L))))))
```

In order to write essentially any useful C program, we must have knowledge of the various functions and typedef'ed datatypes, and so forth defined in various system header files that we "include" within the program files to make use of.

The "include-file" infrastructure of C is one of the most intricate and difficult parts of the C language. There are many built-in functions in C such as *ioctl* or *pow* that we may want to use. First, it is often difficult to learn about these functions, some of which will be particular to the operating system and CPU chip being used. Although Internet searches (and the man command on Linux/Unix systems) are helpful, there is no substitute for a good manual, which can be hard to come by.

Second, the header-file "structure" for a multiplatform compiler like the GNU Compiler Collection (GCC) is extremely complex. There is a system-specific sequence of directories known to the compiler that is searched in order for the requested header-files. Determining this sequence is difficult, although a web search will generally yield a few useful tips among a mass of partly erroneous posts. Since individual header-files contain "includes," referring to "downstream" header-files, and header-files with the same name occur in different directories in the search sequence, it can be hard to find a header-file relevant to some function or symbol we want to know about, and it is even harder to *read* a header-file to learn about the functions and/or other objects defined therein. This problem is compounded by the obscuring of "datatypes" within header-files, by the naming choices intended to minimize the "collision" with names chosen by programmers, and by numerous "ifdef" constructions introduced to deal with various operating systems and CPUs.

In the *lisp.c* file, the command "#include linuxenv.h" specifies that the file *linuxenv.h* be sought, first in the directory where the file *lisp.c* containing the referencing include-command resides (where it should, in fact, be found), and then in the system-specific sequence of directories. In the include-file *linuxenv.h* we have the include statements that load the needed definitions of the various built-in C functions and other objects that are used in *lisp.c*; it is quite likely that you will need to fiddle with this file to get *lisp.c* to compile on your system.

Here is the *linuxenv.h* file used in the LISP Interpreter program above for a Linux environment using the GCC compiler.

```
/* file: ~/lisp/linuxenv.h */
/* This is the environment header file for the GNU C compiler on intel 386
   linux.
   This file is to contain any machine and compiler specific definitions. */

#include <stdlib.h>
#include <stdio.h>
#include <signal.h>
#include <setjmp.h>
#include <math.h>
#include <fcntl.h>
#include <memory.h>
#include <sys/stat.h>
#include <sys/file.h>
#include <string.h>
#include <strings.h>
#include <time.h>
#include <sys/time.h>
#include <sys/types.h>
#include <sys/errno.h>
#include <sys/ioctl.h>
#include <sgtty.h>
#include <stdarg.h>
#include <values.h>

/* end of linuxenv.h */
```

> **Exercise 29.1:** The C language passes procedure arguments by value, that is, a copy of each actual argument is passed (stored in a location on the stack used for arguments, local variables, and return addresses). Also, arguments can be assigned values within a procedure; in the case of a copy argument, this merely changes the copy. Use this device and add code to the *gc* procedure that looks ahead from a node *p*, and avoids recursively calling *gc* when at most one of the nodes A_p or B_p needs to be marked. What benefits can be expected from using this code?

Exercise 29.2: Program the entire LISP interpreter to run on an available LISP system. Some trickery will be needed to make your interpreter conform to the GOVOL dialect of the LISP language given in this book.

Exercise 29.3: Reprogram the LISP interpreter given here to solve the problem that the list-area, the atom table, and the number table have fixed sizes. Devise methods for allocating and using more space for these data structures when they become full rather than failing as the program above does now.

Of course, for modern paging systems, we might be able to specify that these areas be very large, but only use part of the space for such a data area initially, secure in the knowledge that pages that are never accessed, never exist until they are accessed. This still leaves the problem of rehashing for the atom table.

One can imagine that a suitable cooperative paging system might make it possible to request that certain data areas be started on a new page in the logical address space and occupy a block of contiguous pages at the end of the allocated memory, and that such a data area is accessed only through a pointer, and that we can ask for such access to be extended in size by some integral number of pages, and that all the address variables for these extensible areas be appropriately reset. In this exercise, however, you should not assume any help, and only use the basic C *malloc* routines.

Below is a `Makefile` for compiling and linking the LISP Interpreter program on a Linux system. The input is the source code file `lisp.c` together with the header file `linuxenv.h`. The output is the executable program file `lisp`. The command to compile `lisp.c` is: [`make -f Makefile lisp`].

```
# file: Makefile                        date: 1/3/2017
#
# This file is a control file for the make program. It contains the
# specifications for building the lisp executable program, lisp, from
# the C source file lisp.c using the GNU C-compiler on linux. To build
# the lisp executable file , lisp, type 'make lisp' after the operating
# system prompt in the appropriate directory where lisp.c and linuxenv.h
# reside.

# CFLAGS is a macro for certain flags that can be passed to the compiler.
# The flag -g tells the compiler to include debugging information
# in the resulting executable; the flag -O means use the lowest
# level of compiler optimizations. CFLAGS is not currently used in this
# makefile.
CFLAGS=-g -O
```

```
# CC is a macro for the C-compiler used in compile and link commands.
CC=gcc

# The following line begins with the name of the target (i.e. the file
# to be constructed), lisp.o, and then lists the file(s) on which it
# depends--the C source file lisp.c. The next line is the command for
# compiling the C source file in order to construct the file lisp.o; the
# flag -c means only compile--do not link--the named C file, and the
# flag -o lisp.o means name the output file lisp.o.
lisp.o: lisp.c
$(CC) -c -o lisp.o lisp.c

# The following line begins with the name of the target, lisp, which
# is an executable file, and then lists the file on which it
# depends--the object file lisp.o. The next line is the command for
# linking the object file, lisp.o with all requested library files,
# and producing the output file, lisp. -lm means link-in the math
# library module, libm.o and -lc means link-in the main C library
# module, libc.o. There are other libraries that are included by default!
# Note -lm and -lc must occur after lisp.o, and for some versions of
# GCC, you must leave-out -lm and/or -lm.
lisp: lisp.o
$(CC) $(CFLAGS) -o lisp lisp.o -lm -lc
    chmod 777 lisp
# end of Makefile
```

To run the LISP interpreter, we *cd* into the directory where the lisp executable file is kept, and type lisp. Note the file lispinit must also be present in this directory.

> **Exercise 29.4:** The LISP Interpreter program given above is compiled and linked to yield an *executable program*; this program is the file *lisp*, and when ./lisp is typed as a command, the LISP interpreter is run. If you would like to write a LISP *program,* that is, a collection of LISP functions that can be run on demand, you could placed these functions in a text file, say MP, and then run the LISP Interpreter program, *lisp,* and enter the directive @MP to define these functions. Then you would "run" any of these functions as desired.
>
> How might you construct a LISP *compiler* program that would take a text-file containing a collection of LISP-function definitions, including a particular LISP-function named MAIN with no arguments, as input, and produce a LISP "executable" file with a name you specify, say LISPP, that can then be run with the effect that the functions in the input file are defined and the initial function MAIN is called?

Bibliography

[Abr89] Bruce Abramson. Control strategies for two-player games. *ACM Computing Surveys*, 21(2):137–161, June 1989.

[ACR87] John R. Anderson, Albert T. Corbett, and Brian J. Reiser. *Essential Lisp*. Addison Wesley, Reading, MA, 1987.

[All78] John Allen. *Anatomy* of LISP. McGraw-Hill, NY, 1978.

[BB66] E. C. Berkeley and Daniel G. Bobrow, editors. *The Programming Language LISP: Its Operation and Applications*. MIT Press, Cambridge, MA, 1966.

[Bel57] Richard Bellman. *Dynamic Programming*. Princeton University Press, Princeton, NJ, 1957.

[Ers59] Andrey Ershov. *Programming Programme for the BESM Computer*, translated from the Russian original. Pergamon Press, London, 1959.

[Fod79] John Foderaro. *The Franz LISP Manual*. University Press of Califirnia, Berkeley, CA, 1979.

[Fri74] Daniel P. Friedman. *The Little LISPer*. SRA Inc., Chicago, IL, 1974.

[Fri86] Daniel P. Friedman. *The Little LISPer*. SRA Inc., Chicago, IL, second edition, 1986.

[Hof85] Douglas R. Hofstadter. *Metamagical Themas*. Basic Books, NY, 1985.

[Kle52] Stephen C. Kleene. *Introduction to Metamathematics*. D. Van Nostrand Co. Inc., Princeton, NJ, 1952.

[Knu68] Donald Ervin Knuth. *The Art of Computer Programming, Volume 1: Fundamental Algorithms*. Addison-Wesley, Reading, MA, 1968.

[Knu73] Donald Ervin Knuth. *The Art of Computer Programming, Volume 3: Searching and Sorting*. Addison-Wesley, Reading, MA, 1973.

[KnuMo75] D.E. Knuth and R.W. Moore. An analysis of alpha-beta pruning. *Artificial Intelligence*, 6:293–326, 1975.

[Kur81] Toshiaki Kurokawa. A new fast and safe marking algorithm. *Software Practice and Experience*, 11:671–682, 1981.

[Mag79] *Byte Magazine*, August 1979. Issue devoted to LISP.

[McC60] John McCarthy. Recursive functions of symbolic expressions and their computation by machine, part I. *CACM*, 3(4):184–195, April 1960.

[McC61] John McCarthy. A basis for a mathematical theory of computation. *Proceedings of the WJCC*, 19:225-238, 1961.

© Gary D. Knott 2017
G. D. Knott, *Interpreting LISP*, DOI 10.1007/978-1-4842-2707-7

[McC78] John McCarthy. History of LISP. *ACM SIGPLAN Notices*, 13(8), August 1978.

[McC79] John McCarthy. History of LISP. *Stanford A.I. Lab. (draft)*, 1979.

[Mee79] J.R. Meehan. *The New UCI LISP Manual.* Lawrence Erlbaum Associates, Hillsdale, NJ, 1979.

[MIT62] *LISP 1.5 Programmer's Manual*, MIT Press, Cambridge, MA, 1962.

[Moo74] David Moon. *MACLISP Reference Manual, Version 0.* Laboratory for Computer Science, MIT Press, Cambridge, MA, April 1974.

[MSW83] David Moon, Richard Stallman, and Daniel Weinreb. *LISP Machine Manual.* MIT Artificial Intellegence Laboratory, Cambridge, MA, fifth edition edition, 1983.

[NM44] John Von Neumann and Oskar Morgenstern. *The Theory of Games and Economic Behavior.* Princeton University Press, Princeton, NJ, 1980, 1944.

[PT87] Andrew R. Pleszkun and Matthew J. Thazhuthaveetil. The architecture of lisp machines. *IEEE Computer*, March 1987.

[SA83] G. Sussman and H. Abelson. *The Structure and Interpretation of Computer Programs.* MIT Press, Cambridge, MA, 1983.

[Sam79] Hanan Samet. Deep and shallow binding: the assignment operation. *Computer Languages*, 4:187–198, 1979.

[SB60] Klaus Samelson and Friedrich L. Bauer. Sequential formula translation. *Communications of the ACM*, 3(2):76–83, 1960.

[Sik76] Laurent Siklossy. *Let's Talk LISP.* Prentice-Hall, Englewood Cliffs, NJ, 1976.

{Sl63] J.R. Slagle. Game trees, M&N minimaxing, and the M&N alpha-beta procedure. A.I. Group Report No. 3, Lawrence Radiation Laboratory, Livermore, CA.

[SlDi69] J.R. Slagle and J.K. Dixon. Experiments with some programs that search game trees. JACM, 16(2):189–207, April 1969.

[SlDi70] J.R. Slagle and J.K. Dixon. Experiments with the M&N tree-searching program. CACM, 13(3):147–155, March 1970.

[Sta89] Richard W. Stark. *LISP, Lore. and Logic.* Springer-Verlag, NY, 1989.

[Ste84] Guy L. Steele Jr. *Common Lisp.* Digital Press, DEC, Billerica, MA, 1984.

[Tha86] Matthew J. Thazhuthaveetil. *A Structured Memory Access Architecture for LISP.* PhD thesis, University of Wisconson, August 1986. Ph.D. thesis, CS report 658.

[Tou84] David S. Touretzky. *LISP-A Gentle Introduction to Symbolic Computation.* Harper & Row, NY, 1984.

[Wan84] Mitchell Wand. What is LISP? *American Mathematical Monthly*, 91(1):32–42, January 1984.

[Wei67] Clark Weissman. *LISP 1.5 Primer.* Dickenson, Belmont, CA, 1967.

[WH89] Patrick Henry Winston and Berthold K.P. Horn. *LISP.* Addison-Wesley, Reading, MA, first edition 1981, second edition 1984, third edition 1989.

[Whi79] Jon L. White. Macsyma symbolic manipulation program. In *Proceedings of the 1979 MAC-SYMA Users' Conference*, Cambridge, MA, 1979. MIT Laboratory for Computer Science.

[Wil84] Robert Wilenski. *LISPcraft.* W.W. Norton & Co., NY, 1984.

Index

A

Algorithmic ideas, 91
APPEND function, 47–48
APPLY function, 78
Asymmetric valuation, 102
ATOM predicate, 27
Atom table
    function (*see* Functions)
    number atoms, 5
    ordinary atoms, 3, 5
    pictorial notation, 23–26

B

Bind actual and formal arguments
    Algol lexical scoping, 68
    association list, 67
    binding times, 69
    call-time binding, 70
    dotted-pairs, 67
    dynamic scoping, 67
    λ-expression, 67
    EVAL, 72
    free variable, 68
    functional argument
        problem, 69, 70
    function/special form, 68
    macros, 73
    shallow binding, 71
    skip-binding, 69
    variation, 71
    versions, 71
Blank character. *See* Space character
BODY function, 55
BOXPOS function, 104

C

CAR function, 27–28
CDR function, 27–28
CONS function, 27–28
C program
    LISP in, 110–134
        ASCII text, 120–122
        eaL list, 127–128
        end of file, 120
        number table, 122–123
        sread procedure, 117–118
        statement replacement, 125–126
        static variables, 124–125

D

DEEPENOUGH function, 104
DIFFERENCE function, 11
DIFF function, 97–99
DO function, 77
Dot-notation, 36
Dotted-pair notation, 35

E

ELIST function, 95–97
End of file (EOF), 120–122
EQ predicate, 14
EQUAL predicate, 49
EVAL function, 12
Evaluation operator, 9–10
Experimental programs, 91
λ-expression, 43
    binding data, 43
    DEFINE/DEFUN, 44

© Gary D. Knott 2017
G. D. Knott, *Interpreting LISP*, DOI 10.1007/978-1-4842-2707-7

λ-expression (*cont.*)
    FACT, 44
    impredicative definition, 44
    SETQ, 44

▓ F

FACTORS function, 80
Fair game, 101
FLOOR function, 12
Forms
    AND, 39
    COND, 39
    OR, 39
FORTRAN, 91
FPRINT function, 97
FSET function, 95
Functions, 6
    built-in, 7
    dotted-pair, 28
    domain values, 6
    expression, 7
    forms
        lists, 11–12
        NIL, 13
        predicate, 14–15
        total function, 13
    function-valued atom, 7
    NIL, 7
    range, 6
    special forms, 6
    undefined value, 8

▓ G

Garbage collection
    bindlist list, 135
    disconnected list nodes, 137
    gc and newloc procedure, 135
    number table, 135–136
GENMOVES function, 107
GETPROP function, 86
GREATERP function, 61

▓ H

Hashing, 121
Hash value, 121
HPICK functions, 107

▓ I, J, K

INTO function, 77

▓ L

LABEL special form, 57
LAMBDA. *See* λ-expression
LESSP function, 61
linuxenv.h file, 141
LISP
    data values, 1
    functions, 1
    GOVOL, 1
    interpreter program, 1
        C, 110–124, 126–134
        form, 109
        subroutines, 109
    unique features, 1
lispinit file, 139
List notation
    built-in function, 38
    dot-notation, 36
    dotted-pair
        notation, 35
    partial function, 38
    pure list, 37
    S-expressions, 35, 37
    total function, 38

▓ M

MACRO function, 73
Makefile file, 142–143
Minimal LISP, 75–76
MINUS function, 12

▓ N

Nonatomic
    S-expressions, 17, 21, 36
NOT function, 61
NULL function, 61
NUMBERP predicate, 14
Number table
    data types, 4
    floating-point numbers, 3, 7
    function (*see* Functions)
    pictorial notation, 23

■ O

ONTO function, 78
Ordinary atoms, 5–7

■ P

Perfect-information game, 101, 103
Pictorial notation
    atom table, 23–26
    number table, 23
    S-expression, 24
    typed-pointer, 23
PLUS function, 7, 11
POWER function, 12
Predicates, 14–15
PRINT function, 83
PRINTCR function, 83
PRODUCT function, 77
Properties, 85
    GETPROP, 86–88
    g-property value, 85
    property list, 85
    PUTPROP, 85–88
    REMPROP, 86–88
    RPLACA and RPLACD, 88
    TCPROP, 88
Pure list, 37
PUTPROP function, 85

■ Q

Quote/apostrophe symbol, 59
QUOTE form, 11, 18
QUOTIENT function, 12

■ R

READ pseudo-function, 83
Recursive functions, 57
REMPROP function, 86
REVERSE function, 48
RPLACA function, 88
RPLACD function, 89

■ S

SETQ form, 6, 11
S-expressions, 109
    arguments, 75
    definition, 17

dot notation, 17
dotted-pair, 17
list notation, 35, 37
not operators, 17
pictorial notation, 24
QUOTE, 18
typed-pointers, 31
Space character, 5
Special form
    EVALQUOTE, 54
    QUOTE, 59
    SET, 55
    SETQ, 57
    SETQQ, 54
    SPECIAL, 53
    substitution, 53
    unnamed functions, 55
Sread procedure, 109, 117–118
Statistical methods, 105
SUM function, 77
Swrite procedure, 109
Symbolic differentiation
    DIFF, 93, 95, 97–99
    differentiation rules, 94
    E-expressions, 94
    ELIST function, 95–97
    forms, 93
    FPRINT, 95, 97
    FSET, 95
    infix form, 93
    MKATOM function, 93
    real-valued function, 93

■ T, U, V

Terminal positions
    $\alpha\beta$ algorithm, 105, 107–108
    box, 101
    circle symbol, 101
    coroutines, 107
    dotted-pair, 104
    dynamic ordering, 107
    game tree, 102
    GENMOVES function, 107
    hypotheses, 102
    maximizing player, 102
    minimaxing, 102
    PICK function, 103
    pitch positions, 108
    planning/decision-making, 103
    representations, 104

Terminal positions (*cont.*)
  skip-binding function, 105–106
  static valuation function, 104
  Von Neumann and
      Morgenstern, 102–103
TIMES function, 12
Total function, 13
Typed-pointers, 64
  built-in function, 64
  dotted-pairs, 20, 31
  floating-point value, 19
  function, 32
  integer index, 19
  nonatomic S-expression, 21

S-expressions, 31
typecode, 19
type-field and value-field, 19
unnamed special form, 64
untyped-pointer, 20

■ W, X, Y

WHILE statement, 80–81

■ Z

ZEROP predicate, 14
Zero-sum game, 101–102

Get the eBook for only $5!

Why limit yourself?

With most of our titles available in both PDF and ePUB format, you can access your content wherever and however you wish—on your PC, phone, tablet, or reader.

Since you've purchased this print book, we are happy to offer you the eBook for just $5.

To learn more, go to http://www.apress.com/companion or contact support@apress.com.

Apress®

Printed in the United States
By Bookmasters